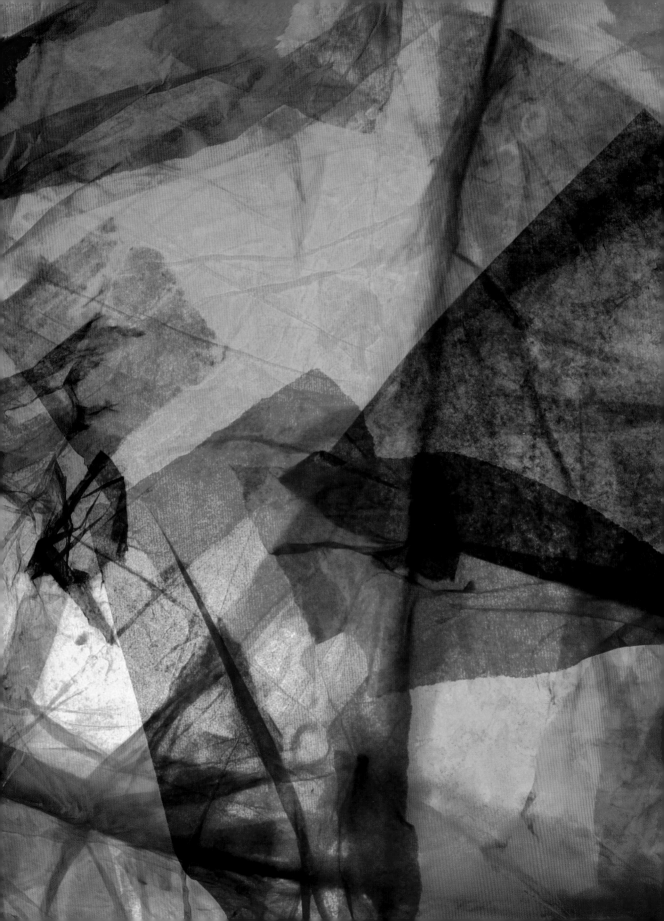

MAKE IT WILD!

101 THINGS TO MAKE AND DO OUTDOORS

Jo Schofield and Fiona Danks

F

FRANCES LINCOLN LIMITED
PUBLISHERS

FOR CONNIE, DAN, EDWARD, HANNAH AND JAKE

Frances Lincoln Ltd
4 Torriano Mews
Torriano Avenue
London NW5 2RZ
www.franceslincoln.com
www.goingwild.net

Make it Wild!
Copyright © Frances Lincoln 2010
Text copyright © Fiona Danks and Jo Schofield 2010
Photographs copyright © Jo Schofield and Fiona Danks 2010

First Frances Lincoln edition: 2010

Fiona Danks and Jo Schofield have asserted their right to be identified
as the authors of this work in accordance with the Copyright, Designs
and Patents Act 1988 (UK).

A catalogue record for this book is available from the British Library.

ISBN 978-0-7112-2885-6

Designed by Sarah Slack

Printed and bound in China

9 8 7 6 5 4 3 2

This book includes some potentially dangerous activities. Please note that any reader,
or anyone in their charge, taking part in any of the activities described does so at their
own risk. Neither the author nor the publisher can accept any legal responsibility for
any harm, injury, damage, loss or prosecution resulting from the use or misuse of the
activities, techniques, tools and advice in the book.

It is illegal to carry out any of these activities on private land without the owner's
permission; and it is imperative to obey all laws relating to the protection of land,
property, plants and animals.

CONTENTS

MAKE IT WILD! 8

EPHEMERAL ART 14
Beach art 18
Woodland art 26
Ice and snow 32

OUTDOOR TOYS 46
Wooden go-carts 50
Cricket and rounders bats 54
Boats and rafts 56
Planes and gliders 60
Kites 62
Flaming balloons 66

MAKE IT FROM CLAY 70
Working with wild clay 74
Firing clay 82
Smoke decorating 86

MAKE IT FROM WOOD 90
Rustic furniture 94
Driftwood sculptures 98
Twig sculpture 100
Wild baskets 102
Withy lanterns 106

NATURE'S PIGMENTS 110
Natural paints 114
Natural dyes 120

NATURAL CRAFTS 126
Jewellery 130
Paper making 134
Leaf plates and bowls 140
Bulrush dolls 142
Pewter casting 144
Felting 146
Making a leather purse 150
Natural mobiles and windchimes 152

FURTHER INFORMATION 154
Discovering more about
  how to make it wild 156
Leaving no trace 156
Fire safety 156
Tool safety 156
Further information about
  creative outdoor activities 157

Index 158
Acknowledgements 160

MAKE IT WILD!

**Anyone wanting a quiet walk on that blustery autumn
afternoon would have been in for a bit of a shock.
The woods rang out with the excited shrieks and crazy
laughter of five elaborately decorated young warriors.
Armed with sticks, they were ready to defend their
territory to the bitter end and alarm innocent passers-by
with their scary painted faces. This was a real
adventure, an escape into a world of stories and
dreams, all made possible by a bit of crushed chalk.**

Only an hour earlier those young warriors had been sprawled in front of the television, squabbling over the computer and refusing to budge off the sofa. How could we ever tempt them away and channel all that pent-up energy into something positive? We grabbed a pestle and mortar, a few paintbrushes and a bottle of water, and dragged everybody off to the woods. We easily gathered some chalk from upturned tree roots and before long everyone was grinding it into a fine powder, and then mixing it into a smooth white paste with a little water. Stripping off their T-shirts – no one complained about the cold – the children decorated their faces, arms and even bodies with intricate patterns and pictures inspired by Aboriginal designs. With no further prompting they had been transformed into imaginary characters and were dashing off into the woods. A rather dull half-term afternoon had become a memorable experience.

We believe in letting the wild world weave its magic on young people. Wild places have a unique capacity to release a sense of adventure, stimulate imaginations, unleash creativity and restore a sense of wonder. Our families have wiled away many hours in local woods, distant mountains and back gardens. We have invented games, made weird and wonderful sculptures, raced miniature leaf boats down streams and collected natural treasures to turn into keepsakes. *Make it Wild!* draws on these experiences, aiming to inspire young people to get

off their backsides, forget about their image, leave commercial toys and games behind for a while and go in search of some active, inexpensive entertainment in the great outdoors.

The wild world is ripe with endless possibilities for play, creativity and discovery. After a two-hour walk to a remote Hebridean beach where there wasn't a plastic beach toy or electronic game in sight, everyone was forced to search around for something to do. Sitting idly trickling dry sand between her fingers, Hannah began to experiment. Placing one hand down flat on the smooth damp sand, she poured dry sand all around it; when she lifted her hand she revealed a perfect silhouette. Soon everyone joined in, producing a scene reminiscent of ancient cave paintings created by spitting mouthfuls of paint around hands placed on the rock walls. That wild and empty beach had become a place full of exciting new ideas. In this fast-moving, quick-fix modern world, in which many children expect to have their needs met immediately, nature helps us all slow down a little and realize that less is often more.

Make it Wild! is about looking at what nature has to offer in a new light. It's about appreciating the potential of diverse raw materials such as snow, leaves, chalk and sticks and learning how to work with them. It's about discovering how to use nature's free, renewable resources to make anything from a cricket bat or a clay monster to an ice lantern or some leaf paper. (And for those parents and carers who shudder at the thought of messy craft activities in their tidy house – take heart, and just get everyone outdoors!)

Outdoor crafts can show children that technology is not just about pressing the keys on a keyboard but can be about making something that is practical and useful, like a home-made go-cart for whizzing down a hill, or a clay pinch pot you can eat out of. Such activities may take a long time, and they may be difficult; but we have found that young people value the finished products all the more for having made them themselves, and feel a sense of pride in the achievement. This not only brings them closer to nature but also connects them to ancient civilizations and technologies.

The outdoors also offers young people time and space for exploration, for learning by mistakes and for working together. Making things outdoors involves exercising creativity and imagination, solving practical problems, seeing a process through from start to finish, and learning to judge risk. These experiences help children think for themselves, develop a commonsense understanding of the way things work, and keep safe; they prepare them for the real world. Group activities such as a family boat-making competition or gathering round a fire telling scary stories can take them away from the solitary virtual world of networking and surfing the web and help nurture real connections with family and friends.

We believe that everyone has buried desires to reconnect with nature and discover wildness; and we know from experience that once young people are out there they will come up with all sorts of ingenious ideas and have a great time. But the hardest part is getting them out of the door. How do you tempt young people to get outside? One solution, we have found, is to remove barriers – by making time for outdoor play and putting it higher up the priority list. Another lies in making experiences in the natural world as exciting, challenging, varied and inspiring as possible. We hope that the activities in *Make it Wild!* might make it easier to encourage children to get outdoors and have fun.

Of course today's young people must grow up with an understanding and appreciation of modern technology, but an ever-increasing reliance on multi-channel TV and computers encourages a passive indoor lifestyle. A downside of a culture that bombards us with commercial messages promoting the acquisition of the latest toys, fashions and gadgets is that it suggests that happiness depends on these things; and it is a wasteful one too, where the art of making things is in danger of being lost. We hope that *Make it Wild!* will redress the balance and help reunite young people with the natural world in all its vitality, its freedom, its opportunities, its intensity and its inspiration. Perhaps it will encourage everyone to discover their inner wildness. We hope that it might also help the next generation develop important life skills and forge a deeper link with wild places, for if they come to value everything that such places have to offer they will surely want to protect them for future generations.

EPHEMERAL ART

BEACH ART

WOODLAND ART

ICE AND SNOW

EPHEMERAL ART

Have you ever spent hours making the most perfect sand castle? Perhaps it was embellished with a deep moat and sculpted turrets, fortified with smooth serpentine walls, decorated with shells and crowned with a flag. And did the castle's inevitable destruction by the advancing tide destroy all that enjoyment? Probably not – in fact perhaps racing against the tide while building and then watching the waves erode the castle bit by bit made the whole project even more fun.

Wild ephemeral art is all about using natural materials creatively within their surroundings and then allowing them to return to nature. Perhaps you are wondering why anyone should spend ages creating a masterpiece only to watch it disappear. But what about cooking a meal or tending a garden? A meal that takes hours to prepare may be consumed in minutes, while a carefully tended plant may bloom for only a day, but no cook or gardener would say that either was any less worthwhile for that. Indeed, perhaps the fact that its existence is fleeting is what makes ephemeral art so compelling: you enjoy it right now because it may be gone by tomorrow.

Creating ephemeral art is something anyone can do, but it needs time: time to become absorbed in a particular place, discover its mood and the materials it offers, and then create whatever these inspire. The art is to use only what you find and make something that works within the landscape. Use things you might not have considered before. Discover the potential of stones on a beach, of ice on frozen puddles or of piles of coloured leaves. You can even use intangible things such as the wind or the rain. Nature is dynamic, subject to change over time and with the elements; by making ephemeral art you become more aware of the influence of weather, growth, decay, tides or the flow of water. Photographing your creations is a great way of using modern technology to capture the moment.

BEACH ART

Every beach has something special to use for ephemeral art - sand, stones, shells, rocks, seaweed, water, and of course the relentless tide. Work below the tide line has to be done quickly: you may not even have time to complete your masterpiece as the sea approaches.

SAND SILHOUETTES

Hannah stumbled across this simple idea while letting dry sand trickle through her fingers (see page 10); making hand silhouettes quickly evolved into making full-body silhouettes. Someone would lie down on the darker, flatter, damp sand, shutting their eyes tight while the others poured dry sand all around their body; then the challenge was for each model to stand up without spoiling their silhouette. Have a go at making silhouettes with hands, feet, toys to create a collage of silhouettes. Collect dry pouring sand from well above the high-tide mark. Put it in a bucket or bag and take it below the high-tide line to make the silhouettes.

SAND PAINTING

Not content with the relatively crude technique of making sand silhouettes, Hannah experimented with other ways of using sand. She filled a sock with dry sand and by letting it trickle through a small hole she found she could use it rather like paint. Soon she had 'painted" a series of pictures on the darker sand near the sea (see page 16).

To make your own sand pictures, collect dry sand in a bucket and make yourself a pouring bag out of a sock, a vest, a plastic bag, a bottle – whatever you can find. Alternatively, try roughing up damp sand with a beach rake or even your fingers or toes, using the contrast between rough and smooth sand to make pictures.

SAND SCULPTURES

We have sculpted mermaids, turtles, fish and horses – all you need is sand, a bit of imagination and perhaps a few natural tools such as razor shells or bits of driftwood.

The sand should be damp but not sloppy. First make a rough mound of sand and pat it firmly into a basic shape – patting presses air out of the sand, making it stronger. Then add details, starting in the middle and working out to the edges to avoid working across completed sections. Use a shell or a stick to add the finer details – and a straw comes in handy for blowing sand out of awkward nooks and crannies.

SHELL PICTURES

It was a bitter wintry day and the adults were ready to leave the beach and get to the pub and its welcoming fire. But Connie and Ama were in a frantic race against the tide. Would they finish their shell serpent before it was washed away? They weren't going anywhere until it was completed. So the adults caved in and started gathering shells. The last shell was added in the nick of time, along with a seaweed tongue as the finishing touch.

STONE PICTURES

On the remote Scottish isle of Colonsay we spotted the vast outline of a whale, clearly defined in grey stones on a grassy slope near the beach. This landscape-scale picture was the work of the conceptual artist Julian Meredith and a team of volunteers. Made entirely of locally gathered pebbles, it was never finished because the artist wanted visitors to this wild spot to make their mark by adding more pebbles, rather as walkers often feel compelled to add a stone to a cairn on a mountain summit. We played our part and added more stones when we walked past. But stone art doesn't have to be on such an enormous scale. You can try something a little less ambitious at the beach, by a river or lake or even beside a mountain path.

PEBBLE PATTERNS

Dan was intrigued to find some pebbles bisected by white lines. He collected as many as he could find and made a spiral, carefully matching up the lines. Some beaches are littered with pebbles of every shape, size and colour, perfect for ephemeral art.

● Collect different-coloured pebbles and find a spot to make a mosaic. This could be on the sand, on a large rock or on grassland above the beach.

● Sort the pebbles into categories – sizes, colours, shapes.

● Using a stick draw the outline of a picture or a pattern on sand or ground and then fill it in with pebbles. Maybe it could be split into sections so that each person has their own little bit to complete.

STONE TOWERS

Lucas and Connie were determined to make the tallest stone tower ever! Using a large level rock as the base, they took time to choose exactly the right flat stones and secured each layer before moving on to the next one. They discovered that small pebbles placed around and under each stone helped to stabilize the structure. As the tower rose, each layer was slightly smaller than the previous one. Eventually Connie had to scramble up on to Lucas's shoulders to add the last few stones. Their handiwork stood like a beacon until the incoming waves toppled it into the sea.

Plan and construct stone towers with care so they won't fall down; destroy them before leaving the beach.

STONE CAIRNS

We had fun making small cairns on the shoreline and then watching to see how long they survived the power of the incoming waves. Alternatively, you could make them higher up the beach and put night lights inside them, or make them in places you like – perhaps to mark a favourite view or a special spot where you like to sit.

SHADOW ART

The north Norfolk beach was bathed in low sunlight that March afternoon. Remembering how many photographs of ephemeral art use low sunlight to accentuate shapes and contrasts, we gathered small razor shells and stuck them end on into the sand to make long shadows. We experimented with making patterns, happy to fiddle about and enjoy the glorious golden light. Although shadow art could work in a variety of settings, sandy beaches are perfect, with their smooth surface yet soft consistency. The moment will pass quickly, so do take a camera along with you to record your work.

STONE SCULPTURES

The Canadian Inuit have a tradition of building stone figures on beaches. These ancient symbols, called inukshuk, are used as landmarks, navigation aids and symbols of friendship and welcome. They are often made in a human form with outstretched arms. Inukshuk can be small or large, a single rock, several rocks balanced on each other, round boulders or flat. A friend, Bill, came across this one, which was 2m/6ft high, and a permanent structure fixed with concrete. Smaller ones are more typical and more achievable. Try making your own stone figures in strategic positions – they need be only a few centimetres/inches. What character can you make?

Eighteen-year-old Lucas was probably feeling rather squashed beneath this voluptuous stone mermaid with flowing seaweed locks (and he will never forgive us for publishing this photograph!). The younger teenagers giggled wickedly at their creation, knowing that poor Lucas couldn't move. Have a go at using stones to create figures and creatures; but preferably not with a real person underneath.

Safety and legal tips

- Making stone towers and sculptures can be dangerous if not well planned. Make sure that there are adults around and check that each stone layer is secure before adding the next one.
- Destroy towers before you leave the beach, if the tide hasn't already done so.
- It is illegal to remove quantities of pebbles from the beach.

RUBBISH SCULPTURES

Sadly, many shorelines are littered with manmade materials such as plastic, rope and nets. How about putting this detritus to good use, by combining it with driftwood and pebbles to create sculptures that mimic or even enhance nature?

Some years ago we scrambled over a cliff to our favourite hidden beach to find that someone had collected all the flotsam and jetsam together and, instead of leaving it in a hideous pile, created a fantastic life-size horse, complete with broken flip-flop tongue. Since then it's become a family tradition to scour beaches for rubbish to transform into scary sea monsters or other spectacular sculptures. Dan spent hours making this dragon to guard the beach, working with both natural materials and rubbish. Doing something creative like this is a good way of cleaning up a beach.

Safety tip

- **Take care when collecting rubbish: keep an eye out for sharp objects and make sure that you do not use materials that are contaminated with hazardous chemical waste, tar or oil.**

WOODLAND ART

Woodlands are full of loose materials suitable for transforming into ephemeral creations – millions of multicoloured autumn leaves, sticks and twigs of every shape and size, and the fallen harvest of nuts and seeds. Autumn may be the most inspiring time for woodland art, but there's always something out there to work with. Even with a few sticks you can make a sculpture such as this tree ring; or with a lively imagination you can use a range of materials to make something like a huge dinosaur nest.

LEAF PICTURES

A couple of sharp frosts transform summer's tired green leaves into vibrant yellows, oranges and reds for a few spectacular days and you can use these fleeting colours to create bright and unexpected artworks. The challenge is to only use natural materials – glue and tape are definitely not allowed! Water will stick leaves to a surface while also enhancing the colours. Or try natural pins such as the thorns of the blackthorn, which are so sharp that they were used in the past for piercing holes in leather.

LEAF FLAMES

Inspired by the fissured trunk of a Scots pine tree, we cut coloured leaves in half and pinned them to the bark with thorns. The final piece looked rather like flames snaking up the tree, echoing the bark's pattern and texture.

RAINBOW SNAKE

A winding branch inspired this colourful snake. First we sorted leaves into different colours, ranging from yellow, through orange to red and then crimson. Then we fixed them to the bark with natural pins, making sure they all overlapped and faced in the same direction. It took only one pin to hold two leaves in place.

Safety tip

- **If using blackthorn pins, watch out for them breaking. If a broken thorn pierces the skin, the wound can occasionally go septic.**

LEAF PICTURES

Ephemeral art is a wonderful way to enhance or emphasize natural patterns and shapes. Look out for a natural feature to use as a starting point for a picture or pattern. We started with a large hollow tree stump, and framed the hole with leaves we had cut in half. As we continued to work, our picture evolved into a sun-like image with rays made from the tips of yellow leaves. Don't worry if you don't know where your art is going – just get stuck in and see what happens.

LEAF POEMS AND MEMORIES

Walking in the woods one day we found a leaf floating in mid-air, halfway between a bare branch and the ground, as if captured in time by a magic spell. Caught on a gossamer thread of spider's silk, it blew this way and that in the breeze. Perhaps we could use leaves to capture moments, and hang them on fine threads from a bare winter tree.

In our leaf collection we found some large magnolia leaves, and used a marker pen to jot down a short poem on each leaf. On an icy morning, when hoar frost clung to each and every little twig, we found a tree that stood alone and tied our leaves to the branches with clear fishing line to make our own poem tree. When we returned a few days later, the leaves were still there but looked quite different bathed in sunlight instead of shrouded in frost – a wonderful reminder of the changing moods of wild places. If you make a poem tree, don't forget to remove the leaves and collect up the fishing line after a couple of days.

On another occasion we made a memory tree. Everyone summed up their favourite outdoor memory in a single word that they wrote on a specially chosen leaf. Then we pinned the leaves to a tree with blackthorn pins.

SUNBEAMS AND SPIDERS' WEBS

Walking through some local woods, the children spotted what looked like sunbeams filtering through the trees. Closer inspection revealed a sculpture of strings spreading out in a tepee shape, each string pegged to the ground with a twig. We made this miniature sunbeam sculpture on the same principle, and then decorated it with natural materials.

On a visit to Groombridge Place Gardens in Kent Connie had spotted giant spiders' webs in the trees. Determined to have a go at making her own smaller version, she made this string web, complete with her very own spider.

Leave no trace

- **Don't make ephemeral art in protected woodlands.**
- **Take care not to gather or damage growing plants. Use only loose materials such as fallen twigs, leaves and fruits.**
- **If using non-natural materials to make a wild sculpture, always take them home with you.**

31

ICE AND SNOW

As I left the house one snowy afternoon, I caught sight of our neighbour's daughter Rose crouched over something. She stood up and took a step backwards to reveal a beautiful snow swan trying to stretch out its wings. It must have taken her ages to compress and sculpt the snow, smoothing it and shaping it. She admitted that she had intended to make a dog but it had evolved into a swan, but she was clearly delighted with the result, even if her hands were freezing!

Snow and ice transform winter's grey darkness into a thrilling wonderland full of exciting possibilities. When we get a rare snowy day our teenagers are always desperate to get outside and make the most of the snow while it lasts. One Christmas when everything was frozen for days on end, we experimented with making our own ice. We left containers of water outside overnight and the next day Edward discovered an ice glass – good enough to drink his morning juice from. Provided you are wrapped up warm, have some decent gloves and are willing to try things out, ice and snow are perfect for making ephemeral art.

ICE WINDOWS

One frosty morning Connie and Kate discovered a thick layer of ice in a bucket. Lifting the ice disc up high, they looked through their wintry window. A couple of trapped leaves gave us the idea of making natural stained-glass windows.

● Pour some water into a bucket or large bowl.

● Fold an 0.5m/18in length of string in half, hang the loop outside the bowl and then place the two loose ends around the inside of the bowl, as shown.

● Gather coloured leaves and winter flowers and arrange them in the water. You want them to be trapped on the surface, so either use materials that float or just put a small amount of water in the bottom of the bowl.

● Leave outside overnight. Ice windows form when it's not quite cold enough for the water to freeze solid. In very cold weather, just put a shallow layer of water in the bottom of a bowl or bucket.

● The next morning remove the ice window – pour a little warm water, over the sides of the bowl to loosen the ice.

● Hang your window up on a branch and enjoy it until the weather warms up. It may melt a little during the day and then freeze again at night, so you can watch how it changes.

ICE BLOCKS

When it's cold enough for water to freeze solid you can have a go at making ice blocks. Fill a plastic container with water. Then tie one end of a piece of string on to something heavy, such as a stone, and let it sink to the bottom so that it will be trapped in the ice. Leave the other end of the string hanging outside the container. Put natural decorative items such as leaves and flowers in the water and leave it all to freeze. Remove the ice block from the container and hang it up outside.

ICE DECORATIONS

Hannah had a vision of a row of ice baubles hanging from the trees – Christmas decorations with a difference. She fiddled about with Plasticine and was delighted to make this heart-shaped ice decoration. She used a small plastic heart as a mould, but you could also try using natural objects such as shells or acorns.

What you need
- Plasticine
- A tray
- Shapes to make moulds
- Fishing line or fine wire

Making the decorations
- Work the Plasticine in your hands until it becomes soft and pliable.
- Place lumps of worked Plasticine on the tray and then press the shapes into each one to make moulds.
- Pour water into each mould.
- Cut a length of fishing line or fine wire for each mould and place it so that about 2.5cm/1in of it is submerged in the mould.
- Place the tray of moulds outside on a cold night, or in the deep freeze.
- When the water has frozen, remove your ice decorations and hang them from a tree or outside a window.

ICE SCULPTURES

Hannah and Connie experimented with ice sculpting, concentrating so hard that they didn't even notice their freezing fingers. This activity needs very cold weather and a degree of patience – ice pieces don't stick instantly because they have to actually freeze together – but wrap up warm and have a go.

● Smash a large slab of ice into fragments.
● Decide where to make your sculpture – a smooth level surface, perhaps, or somewhere it will make an impact. This ice arch was built on an ice table made from a bucket of water that had frozen at the bottom and sides but not in the middle.

● Rub a piece of ice between your hands until it begins to melt, and then put it in position. Choose another piece of ice, melt the surface and start to build your sculpture. You could melt the ice a little in warm water instead of using your hands.
● Continue to build, placing just a few pieces at a time. Leaving your sculpture and working on another project while each piece freezes solid makes it much easier to build. We made this ice arch over a couple of days, but it lasted for almost a week.

OUTDOOR ICE LANTERNS

A friend from Finland, all too familiar with making the most of long dark winters, once told us about ice lanterns. She conjured up a picture of magical lights shining out a welcome on the coldest of nights. Since then we had always wanted to make one.

On a cold night we left water outside in various plastic tubs and buckets, and it froze around the walls and bottom of each tub. We placed these cup-like ice containers in strategic positions around the garden and lit a night light in each one. We also made a larger ice lantern on its own stand, by placing three sticks, each about 1m/3ft in length, in a large bucket of water, positioning them so they made a tripod when we took the ice out of the bucket and turned the whole thing upside down.

If the weather doesn't turn cold enough, have a go at making deep-freeze ice lanterns.

You will need
- Two containers of different sizes, so that one fits inside another, and plastic cups if you are making a larger lantern
- Stones to weight down the smaller container
- Leaves or seed heads for decoration
- Night lights or candles

MAKING THE ICE LANTERNS

- Half fill the larger container with water.
- Place the smaller container in the water and weight it down with stones.
- Slide leaves or seed heads down between the bowls as decoration.
- To make a larger lantern for two or more candles, put several plastic cups filled with stones inside a larger container of water.
- Place the prepared container in the deep freeze for 12 to 24 hours, until frozen.
- Turn the mould upside down and pour hot water over it to loosen the ice.
- Place a night light or candle in the lantern and use it outside or as an unusual if short-lived table decoration.

SNOW SCULPTING

Hannah, Edward and Agnes once built a snow woman who, with her huge feet, massive hands clasped around her belly, staring eyes and mullet hair cut, would have felt quite at home in a Wallace and Gromit film. Playing in the snow can be so much more than just building a snowman or throwing snowballs: have a go at using snow in a more imaginative way.

Always use compacted snow for sculpting: either roll giant snowballs or make solid building blocks by compressing snow into large plastic boxes and then turning it out.

Dan made a dragon by lining up snow blocks and filling in the gaps with loose snow. He made the head from another block, carved details with a garden trowel and finally added fearsome ice teeth from a frozen puddle. But it wasn't until after dark that Dan's dragon really came alive, when its eyes began to glint and real fire poured from its mouth …

CARVING SNOW

See what you can make from compacted snow – animals, cartoon characters or even abstract sculptures and shapes. Carve and work the snow with your gloved hands, or use garden tools such as spades or even saws, and use smaller tools such as trowels to add the details. Keep standing back to view your progress, and make sure that your sculpture has a sturdy base – it's tricky making animals or people with skinny legs!

SNOW LANTERNS

A friend's daughter made masses of little snowballs and carefully balanced them on top of each other to make a sculpture. That night we placed night lights on little ledges carved in each snowball. The sculpture looked beautiful when the night lights were lit, but the slightest breeze blew out the flames. So we experimented with improved versions of snow lanterns, and found that the best method is to make reasonably large snowballs and then hollow them out from the top with a trowel or by pushing a cup down into them. When you place a night light inside each one, because the holes are so deep the snow lanterns will glow softly even in a breeze. On one occasion the teenagers carved hollows out of a snowman that had begun to melt and placed night lights inside.

SNOW MAZES AND PICTURES

If it's too cold to stay still, try rolling a snowball to make a snow maze or draw a pattern or picture in the snow – a face, perhaps. Choose a wide open area and start rolling, rocking the ball gently from side to side as you roll it so that it picks up as much snow as possible, leaving a cleared track in its wake. By walking in its path you won't leave any footprints. Plan your route so that it becomes the lines of your picture, pattern or maze.

OUTDOOR TOYS

WOODEN GO-CARTS

CRICKET AND ROUNDERS BATS

BOATS AND RAFTS

PLANES AND GLIDERS

KITES

FLAMING BALLOONS

OUTDOOR TOYS

I vividly remember seeing some Burmese children playing with an ingeniously designed truck constructed from an old packing case and some scrap wheels. To an outsider their environment apparently offered little to play with, but they made the most of what they had, using imagination and teamwork to make toys out of whatever materials they could find. They didn't sit around getting bored: they just worked together to create their own toys to provide hours of fun.

Perhaps children's imaginations work better when they have fewer manufactured toys and access to a range of loose materials. By making their own toys they can also learn new skills, develop their manual dexterity and find out how to use a range of tools. They can discover how things work, develop an ability to solve problems and learn to think creatively.

We believe in encouraging young people to look at materials in a new way and helping them to understand that the best toys are not necessarily those that are expensive, branded and over-packaged. This chapter reminds us that outdoor toys can be made from natural, scrap and recycled materials that cost next to nothing. The most valuable activities and toys are often those which children have been involved with from the outset; they are much more likely to treasure something they have made for themselves. Get immersed in a project that is essentially outside, and then take your new toys off and have some fun on a remote hillside, by a rushing stream or at the park.

WOODEN GO-CARTS

Like so many people of his generation, my father has fond memories of crazy soapbox derbies, when all the local kids careered downhill on rickety go-carts cobbled together from old wooden soapboxes and pram wheels. Health and Safety didn't have much of a say back then; crashes and bumps were taken for granted and scars and scabs were worn with pride.

Go-carts still have a very special appeal. Go-cart kits are available on the internet at considerable expense, but it's more of a challenge and more fun to assemble your own. A friend's sons and their mates spent much of one summer holiday designing and building a go-cart in the alley behind their house. Another friend's son pestered us to include a go-cart in this book; having read somewhere that all he needed was an old pram, he had been begging his mother to help him find one, with little success.

For our simple wooden gravity-driven go-cart, we made a frame from an old wooden pallet. These can be found abandoned on building sites, but never take them without asking first. Much as we liked the idea of using old pram wheels, in reality these can be hard to find, and we decided that if our go-cart was to be strong, new wheels (preferably with roller bearings and a strong metal rod) would be a good investment. Wheels and the rest of the materials we used can be purchased from good hardware or DIY shops.

The young people had some adult help making this go-cart, but they came up with the initial design themselves. It is still knocking around in our garden and is dragged out now and again for a hair-raising ride.

You will need

- An old wooden pallet
- Hammer, handsaw, hand-drill, nails, screws
- 2 fixed axles – we used 2 × 20mm/1in threaded metal bars (about 60cm/2ft or the width of your go-cart) purchased from www.screwfix.com
- 4 U bolts to attach the axles to the pallet
- 4 wheels, preferably with roller bearings (e.g., wheelbarrow or trolley wheels) and a diameter of 15–20cm/6–8in
- 16 locking nuts to thread on to the axle bar (2 either side of each wheel)
- 8 metal washers, to go on each side of the wheels
- 1 coach bolt with a Nylock locking nut
- 2 plastic washers with a diameter of about 8cm/3in, cut from a plastic milk container
- A piece of old rope about 2m/6ft long to steer with

HOW TO MAKE THE GO-CART

- Start by planning your go-cart design and deciding how to cut the pallet up most efficiently. There was a very lively debate about the best way to design our go-cart – it was a great opportunity to work together. To make this go-cart you need a seat, a body beam and a piece of wood for the front steering axle.
- Take the pallet apart, using a hammer and handsaw. This is quite a challenging task, so take care. Hammer any protruding nails in hard until they are flush with the wood's surface. Select the best pieces of wood for the cart.
- We constructed a slatted box for the seat. You should be able to do this without pulling apart too much of the pallet.

We nailed the two longest pieces of wood together to make the main beam, and then slotted this through the seat as shown, fixing it in place with screws. Sit on the seat to try out the length for size, and decide where to fix the steering axle so that your feet can rest comfortably on it.

Cut a length of wood slightly shorter than your metal axle for the front steering axle. We actually cut three pieces of wood the same length and screwed and glued them together for extra strength.

Turn the go-cart over and fix the two threaded metal bars for front and back wheel axles in place with the U bolts.

To attach the wheels to the axles thread two nuts on to an axle, then add a washer, the wheel, another washer and finally two more nuts.

● Drill a hole through the end of the main beam into the middle of the wooden steering axle. Drop your coach bolt through this, making sure that you put a couple of plastic washers between the main beam and the steering axle so that the front wheels can turn freely. Fix off with the Nylock locking nut underneath.

● Finally, attach a piece of rope to each side of the steering axle; you can use a combination of this and your feet to steer the go-cart.

● We didn't add a brake – the appeal of traditional go-carts seems to be fear as much as fun – but if you would like a brake, attach a piece of wood on a screw pivot to the side of the go-cart. When pulled upright, it will dig into the ground.

● Customize with paint to transform it into a mean machine!

Safety tips

Go-carts can go very fast and be dangerous.

● Wear a helmet and make sure you ride with caution.

● Keep well away from roads, traffic and people. Use go-carts in open spaces where there are no hard objects to crash into.

● Grassy slopes are the best places to use them – you can always roll off knowing there will be a reasonably soft landing.

● Avoid very steep hills, and make sure the slope flattens out at the bottom.

CRICKET AND ROUNDERS BATS

On holiday in Cornwall, Jake, Dan and Lucas were kicking around on the beach wondering what to do when they came across bits and pieces of driftwood along the high-tide line. A rounded piece of wood soon became a rounders bat, while from an old plank they fashioned a cricket bat, tying some string around the handle to improve the grip.

They even improvised their own ball by wrapping string and bits of old rubber tyre round and round a small chunk of driftwood. They spent the rest of the afternoon playing games on the beach. It's amazing how much fun you can have when you thought there was absolutely nothing to play with!

On another occasion, not to be outdone, Edward and Tom tried to make a superior cricket bat in the garden. They cut a large piece of willow from a fallen branch near our house, and then spent a very happy afternoon working with potentially dangerous tools.

MAKING A CRICKET BAT

- Find a length of living wood (preferably willow, from which cricket bats are traditionally made) about 20–25cm/8–10in in diameter.
- Look at the wood and decide which end will be the handle.
- Start by cutting off the bark, and then cut away slowly and carefully at the wood to make the rough shape of a cricket bat. Edward and Tom used an axe to do this.
- As the shape begins to emerge, use smaller tools to finish it off before sanding it down.
- Wind some twine very tightly and neatly around the handle and brush with glue to fix it in place.
- Your finished bat will be fine for knocking around with but wouldn't do for a serious game of cricket!

Safety tips

- **Only use sharp tools when adults are around.**
- **Follow the tool safety guidelines on page 156.**

BOATS AND RAFTS

On our family holidays no one is ever content with just sitting around on the beach. If the children aren't active, the arguments and relentless teasing begin, and then no one enjoys themselves. A boat-making competition always tempts both young and old off their backsides by igniting everyone's competitive spirit.

The brief is always the same: design and make a boat or craft of any description from materials scavenged from the surrounding area. Although we allow ourselves to use string and scissors brought from home, they aren't usually required. Once everyone has perfected their boats, the challenge is to see how well they float or, better still, if they are up to racing down a stream – the winner is the one that arrives intact at a pre-arranged spot downstream. The boats are always different and have become more sophisticated and radical as the children have grown older; marks are often given for ingenious design and resourcefulness. It is often the simplest boats that win, so every person, however young, has an equal chance. But the real key to success is to add a weight or keel to keep the boat upright in the water.

The pictures here show the diversity of crafts designed on one Cornish holiday, when every piece of rubbish on the beach was investigated to see if it might become part of a boat. Lucas's Indonesian outrigger, complete with canvas sail, competed with Ben's beautiful mono-hull driftwood yacht with tin keel, feather mast, tiller and rudder. But Dan's less aesthetic, robust tomato-ketchup torpedo boat with polystyrene outriggers pipped them all at the winning post.

MINI RAFT CHALLENGE

Our friend Iain set Hannah and Fiona the challenge of making a raft big enough to float a can of baked beans. The girls tackled this enthusiastically, using a plastic container, two wine bottles and some dowelling, fixed together with string and wire. They added a mast and a paper sail and then took it down to the sea, where they cast it adrift but kept it safely tethered on fishing line. The raft floated very well, thanks to the mast and to the baked beans, which improved stability.

Try the mini-raft challenge for yourselves. Get everyone to make a raft to carry a chosen item – whether it's a tin of beans, a teddy bear or your picnic lunch. Can your raft carry its cargo safely across the water and keep it dry?

FLAMING NIGHT BOATS

One incredibly still summer evening as we walked back after a holiday drink at the pub, the full moon shone on the mirror-calm sea. There wasn't a single breath of wind and it seemed the perfect night to try making night-light boats. As it was an impulse decision we were unprepared, but within minutes Ben was cutting an old juice Tetra Pak in half, pulling out the ends to make two perfect boats. The wax-coated cardboard ensured they were completely watertight. We rummaged in our rucksack to find some night lights (we always carry them with us, winter and summer!) and put them in the bottom of each boat. Although there was no wind, the movement of the tide meant that the boats travelled pretty quickly, so the candles went out, but Ben solved the problem by making a little well out of aluminium foil and pouring lighter fuel into it.

Once lit, the boats flamed like magnificent torches out across the sea.

With the water all around this was relatively safe; however, if you try this you should make sure you know in advance where they will float (so that they don't drift into trees or grasses) and be able to retrieve them afterwards (so that you don't litter the environment).

Safety tips

- **This activity must be supervised by adults.**
- **Only use a small amount of lighter fuel.**
- **Keep the boats tethered on fishing line so that you can retrieve them afterwards.**

PLANES AND GLIDERS

Each Christmas our living room is packed with paper aeroplanes of every shape and size as the children challenge Grandpa to a flying competition. Somehow Grandpa, an experienced engineer, always wins!

One summer we decided to try making more robust planes and gliders to fly outdoors. We searched the kitchen cupboards for materials – including wooden skewers and dowelling, tape, bits of plastic and screws. Best of all was a flyweight envelope stiffener, left over from some package we had received. Despite some initial scepticism, the youngsters became totally immersed in making planes and gliders, but they quickly discovered that it's one thing to

make a nice-looking plane and quite another to make something that flies well. The flying competition wasn't exactly successful, but next time they will pay more attention to aerodynamics. Already they had begun to learn about the need for a weight on the nose and to get the correct wing-to-body ratio – indeed perhaps they learnt more about physics in this practical session than they might have done in a lesson at school.

DESIGN HINTS FOR GLIDERS

- Make a long narrow body/fuselage.
- The wings should be about the same length as the body, but with a larger surface area.
- When attaching the wings, place their leading edge about one-third of the way along the body of the glider.
- There should be a tail for balance.
- You may need to adjust the centre of gravity to improve the flight of your glider. Try experimenting by putting some clay or a nail or screw on the glider's nose.

GLIDER GAMES

Once you've made a glider, try making up a few outdoor games and challenges. Here are some ideas.

- Whose glider can fly through a hoop hung from a tree?
- Hang some balloons from a branch or a fence. Fix a pin or a tack to the nose of each glider with tape or clay. Then have a competition to see which gliders can burst the balloons and from what distance.
- Attach luminous fishing lures or glow sticks to your gliders and fly them in the dark.

KITES

When Connie goes off to fly her kite she's never alone for long. The kite acts like a beacon to other children, and soon the hillside behind our house is singing with excited voices and fluttering kites.

There is some debate as to where kite making and flying originated, but there is certainly a long history of use in China and Japan, where they were traditionally made with bamboo frames and silk sails. The very first kites were probably made from leaves; to this day fishermen in Indonesia and Polynesia sometimes attach their fishing line to a leaf kite so that they can fly the line out to deeper water. Kites have also been used for defence purposes, transport, spying, forecasting the weather and bird scaring, as well as for pleasure and fighting. They can even be used to make musical sounds; the Chinese name for kite translates as wind harp, as the Chinese sometimes attach whistles to the strings.

Our children had heard tales of the fighting kites made by generations of children in Afghanistan and other countries, and of battles so fierce that competitors stuck ground glass on the kite strings to cut down the opposition. These tales inspired them to make their own fighting kites – although we drew the line at ground-glass reinforcement.

MAKING AN INDONESIAN FIGHTING KITE

We made these simple kites from split bamboo and tissue paper. Everybody became completely absorbed in the task, creating a beautiful selection of kites they were keen to fly. The most critical thing about kite making is weight. Use lightweight materials and as little tape and glue as possible – no one wants a perfect-looking kite that's too heavy to fly.

What you need
- Thick bamboo (which is easier to split than thin bamboo); or you could use any light, dry wood
- A sharp knife
- Masking tape
- Tissue paper in different colours
- Watered-down PVA glue (about one part PVA to two parts water)
- Fine fishing line, or very thin cotton thread wrapped round a stick

Making the spars
- Kite spars should bend without snapping and be as thin and light as possible. Hold the bamboo very firmly and split it with a sharp knife by cutting down and away from yourself with a clean follow-through (see the tool safety guidelines, page 156). Apply steady pressure while twisting the knife. Once you have made a split in the wood, you should be able to pull it apart with your fingers. The knife can get stuck on the nodes and then slide quickly down the lengths between, so take great care and do this only under adult supervision.

- Cut the spars. You need two longer spars of equal length (for the trailing edge) and two shorter ones (for the leading edge) of equal length. The leading-edge spars should be approximately four-fifths of the length of the trailing-edge spars.
- Lay the spars out in a diamond shape, and then cut another spar to run the full length of the diamond from the apex of the leading edges (the leading point) to the apex of the trailing edges (the trailing point). Fix the shape together using small pieces of masking tape.
- Finally, cut a thinner length of bamboo to go across the kite in a curve as illustrated.

Making the tissue wing

● Hold one corner of a sheet of tissue paper and brush the watered-down glue on to it, using steady strokes away from you and keeping the paper flat. Use as little PVA as you can.

● Place the kite frame on the glue-coated tissue and make sure that both sides of the frame are covered in the tissue. Hang it up to dry.

● Decorate the kite with coloured tissue cut into shapes and then brushed with the diluted PVA. Don't be tempted to add too much more tissue or PVA – minimal decoration is best. Then hang up to dry again.

● Take a length of line or cotton thread (the bridle) and attach one end at the point where the cross spar crosses the longest spar; this is your first bridle point. Measure the distance between this and the leading point of the kite; your second bridle point should be the same distance from the trailing point. Cut a little slit in the tissue beside the longest spar at the second bridle point and attach the other end of thread here.

● When you are ready to fly the kite, tie the line to the bridle about one-third of the way along from the leading edge, and off you go!

Flying kites

Always fly your kite in a wide-open space, such as a grassy hill or an empty beach. Choose a day with a good steady wind.

Launching your kite

Holding the line in one hand and the kite in the other, stand with your back to the wind. Hold the kite up until it catches the wind; then let it go and gently let out the line as the wind lifts it upwards. If the kite stops catching the wind, pull the line gently: this should help it go higher. Another way to launch your kite is to ask a friend to hold it and walk a few metres downwind from you while you let out the line. When you're ready, ask your friend to release the kite, and then pull on the line to help it gain height. Don't try to launch a kite by running – let the wind do the work.

Keeping the kite flying

● Maintain a steady line tension so that the kite flies evenly.

● If the line goes slack you will lose control, so pull it in a little and help the kite seek out the wind again.

● To move the kite in the direction in which it is pointing, take the line in a fraction; if you wish to change direction, let out some line.

● Always leave some line on your reel.

Landing the kite

● Reel it slowly and steadily towards you, keeping tension on the line at all times so that it doesn't tangle.

OTHER KITE DESIGNS

Not content to make a diamond-shaped kite like the others,
Jake and Anya came up with their own design. The basic
shape was rectangular but it had a curved frame. They
made every effort to keep the kite as light as possible
and it flew beautifully. Other alternatives might include:

● Using plastic bin liners instead of tissue paper.

● A balloon kite – either a plastic bag or a tissue paper
balloon with a circle of thin willow attached around the open
end (see Flaming Balloons, pages 66–9). These are very quick
and easy to make but won't do stunts.

Safety tips

● **Fly kites in wide-open
spaces where there aren't
many people or obstacles.**

● **Don't fly kites near roads
or overhead power lines.**

● **Be aware of wind conditions
– flying kites in very strong
winds can be dangerous.**

● **Match the size of a kite and
the strength of the wind to
the size and strength of the
kite flyer.**

● **Beware of kite lines pulling
on your hands. It can be
advisable to wear gloves.**

FLAMING BALLOONS

Paper fire lanterns have been used for hundreds of years in China and Thailand to mark special occasions. They are made from a bamboo frame and oiled rice paper, with a small candle attached to the base; the rising hot air lifts the lantern high into the air. Also called wish lanterns, they symbolize the release of problems and worries, so are believed to bring good luck. Sometimes hundreds of them are released at special events, filling the sky with flaming balloons – quite a spectacle but rather dangerous. Needless to say, when our children heard about them, everyone was desperate to have a go!

Because we were worried about our fire lanterns flying away and setting fire to something, we decided to tether them. This was rather like holding a helium balloon and we could walk around slowly with our glowing lanterns. This activity is creative, it takes place in the dark and best of all it has that element of danger that appeals to so many teenage boys.

'Wow!' said Dan, unable to contain his excitement as his balloon filled with hot air and soared high up into the night sky. 'You must do this – it's the best thing in the book!'

Only make these balloons on a still evening without a breath of wind.

What you need
● Coloured tissue paper cut into four pieces about 50cm/20in × 75cm/30in
● Pencil and scissors
● Tape and PVA glue
● Lightweight wood – we used thin bendy willow
● Very fine metal wire (not fuse wire – it melts)
● Flammable material (e.g. toilet paper, cotton wool or fluffed-up tampons)
● Methylated spirits
● A heat source (e.g. a small fire or portable barbecue, or a hair dryer)
● Plenty of water in case any balloons catch fire

MAKING THE BALLOONS

- Place the four pieces of tissue exactly on top of each other and then fold them in half lengthwise. You may wish to use different colours.
- Imagine the fold as the centre of the balloon; then, using a pencil, draw a balloon shape towards the loose edges, as illustrated. Cut along the line: when you unfold the paper you should have identical balloon shapes on the four separate sheets.
- Take the top piece of tissue, sheet 1, and lay sheet 2 on top of it. Glue the outside edges together down one side. Fold sheet 2 in half.
- Take sheet 3 and lay it on top of sheets 1 and 2. Glue down the other side so that sheet 1 now has a sheet stuck on to each side. Fold sheet 3 in half so that the loose edges of both sheets are lying directly on top of the glued edges.
- Take sheet 4 and place it on top of all the sheets. Glue its loose edges to the loose edges of sheets 2 and 3. Take care to prevent the whole lot from sticking together in one gluey mess. Once the seams have dried, open it out into a balloon shape.

- Attach a light bendy twig around the bottom of the balloon; we used about 1.5m/5ft of thin dried willow (it had dried for a long time, so was very light). Use a little tape to attach one end of the willow to the tissue about 2.5cm/1in above the base of the balloon. Then gently bend the twig round inside the balloon, taping it in place as you go. Use as little tape as you can – the balloon should be as light as possible. Make a complete circle around the balloon's base, cutting off any excess wood. This whole process is rather tricky – we found it easiest if one person bent the willow and fed it around the mouth of the balloon while another taped it in place, turning the balloon as they worked.

- Fold any excess tissue at the bottom of the balloon over the twig circle and glue it in place all the way round, sealing the twig inside.

- Measure the diameter of the circle and cut two pieces of fine garden wire to a little more than that length. Fix one of these across the open end of the balloon and fix the other at right angles to the first, forming a cross in the centre. This is where the fuel parcel will go.
- Tie some fine thread or fishing line on to the balloon base. This will be the tether, so the longer it is the higher your balloon will go.
- Roll some flammable material such as cotton wool or tissue paper securely around the cross in the wire. Fluffed-up tampons make excellent tinder – they absorb a lot of fuel, so keep burning for longer.
- Holding the balloon upright, gently pour some methylated spirits on to the flammable material.

- Fill the balloon with hot air before you light it so that the sides are puffed out and less likely to catch fire. We made a small fire in an old olive oil tin; it was safely contained, yet generated enough heat to fill the balloon. Alternatively, use a hairdryer or the heat from a barbecue. As you feel the balloon start to rise, light the pad of flammable material, hold the tether and let it fly up into the night sky above you – and don't forget to make a wish!
- When the fuel runs out, the temperature of the air inside the balloon will fall and the balloon will float back down to earth. You may be able to add more fuel and have another go.

Safety tips

This is a magical and exciting activity, but you should adhere to these safety instructions at all times.
- **Never fly fire lanterns when it's windy; wait for a very still evening.**
- **Only fly fire lanterns in a wide-open space. Never use them near roads, dry standing crops, trees, buildings or airports.**
- **Don't attempt to throw the lanterns to launch them. They rise naturally when full of hot air.**
- **We believe it is safest to keep fire lanterns tethered, because even on a calm evening there is a risk that they will go so high that they will reach a slipstream current and get whisked away.**
- **This activity must always be well supervised by an adult.**
- **See fire safety guidelines, page 156.**

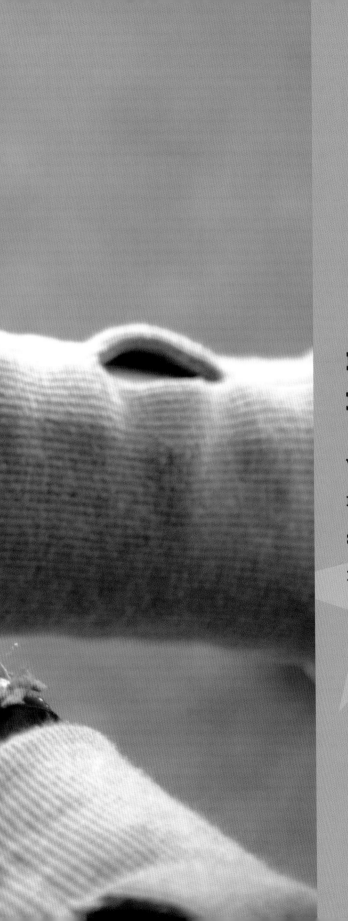

MAKE IT
FROM CLAY

WORKING WITH WILD CLAY

FIRING CLAY

SMOKE DECORATING

PLASTER OF PARIS TILES

MAKE IT FROM CLAY

The boys were all a bit silly to begin with, but after much giggling and messing around, Edward and Clifford decided to make a sculpture of a wild man pooing in the woods. They soon calmed down, becoming totally focused on transforming the lump of clay into an impressive troll-like creature with huge arms and legs and a fearsome face.

Working with clay is the perfect excuse to get your hands dirty. Clay has been made into household and decorative items for the last 6,000 years; it is a real link with the past. Although many young people do get the chance to work with clay, it's usually limited to moulding commercially prepared clay, which is then whisked away to be fired in an electric kiln. We wanted to get back to basics so that everyone could experience the whole process from start to finish – scooping up raw clay from the earth, working it, moulding it and then firing it in an improvised kiln.

Our sculptor friend Carol took us to find natural clay deposits. Armed with buckets and spades, we set off across the fields while the raggle-taggle group of children and teenagers chucked a rugby ball at each other and argued about who should carry the tools. We found grey clay exposed on the sides and bottom of a ditch, and after some initial reticence, everyone jumped in and dug it up with their bare hands. The younger children began moulding straight away, removing sticks and stones and working the clay in their warm hands until it became soft and pliable. Connie made a tiny mouse and a hedgehog with twig prickles, while Hannah made a green man face among some ivy, complete with feather eyebrows and beard. The boys were more interested in chucking clay balls at their sisters but joined in reluctantly when we suggested they make something rude. Before long even they were engrossed, sculpting a grotesque face on a gnarled tree trunk. The afternoon showed the importance of flexibility, of allowing everyone to pursue their own ideas.

WORKING WITH WILD CLAY

Collect raw clay from unpolluted, litter-free ditches.
The better-quality uncontaminated clay is found in
deeper clay beds, which might be exposed at the side
of a stream or by building works. You need to look for
fine workable clay with low organic matter; if you can
roll it into a snake between your palms, it will be
good enough to use. You may need to remove a little
soil to get the clay beneath. Try collecting clay from
different locations to see how much it varies.

PREPARING RAW CLAY

● Take a large handful of raw clay and pick out stones, roots, dead leaves and other debris.

● Work the clay in your hands for several minutes; warmth and motion change clay's consistency, making it pliable and smooth. It may be easier to knead it on a hard surface or a wooden board. If it crumbles, it means that the clay content isn't high enough and you won't be able to mould it. If it sticks to your hands rather than to itself, it's too wet.

● If your local clay isn't pure enough, mix it with water in a bucket and let it settle into layers. Organic material should float to the top, and the finer clay will settle on top of the coarser soil particles. Gently pour the water off and scrape the clay away from the coarser material below.

● We had lots of fun using clay fresh from the ground, but if you can't use it immediately, store in a plastic bag or mix it with water and leave it in a bucket for a few weeks before using. It actually improves with age.

WET CLAY SCULPTURES

While out on a walk we noticed a clay face peeping out at us from the trees. It inspired us to make ephemeral clay art and leave our creations behind for others to discover. This tree with its many branches looked like some multi-armed monster, so we gave it a strange face with a long tongue. Use trees, rocks or other natural features to inspire you, and have a go at creating weird and wonderful clay creatures or patterned sculptures.

● **The green man:** A face surrounded by leaves is a symbol of our unity with the natural world. Try making faces among ivy-covered tree trunks or in other special places in the woods. Can anyone find the faces hiding in the trees?

● **Monsters and giants:** Use the natural features of a tree – textures in the bark or the shapes of the branches – to inspire a monster or a ghoul. Inspiration may also come from characters in favourite books or films –Tolkien's Ents, for example. Make a trail for others to follow – how many monsters can everyone spot?

● **Clay puppets:** Mould clay into heads for puppets as shown opposite.

● **Clay trees and toadstools:** This miniature tree was lovingly made and then decorated with a few autumn leaves, a wet clay sculpture to leave behind in the woods. Try making toadstools to leave behind for fairy folk, or elf houses out of clay.

● **Wet clay tiles:** Line a flat container with cling film or a rag, and then press clay into it to make a tile. Collect natural objects and push them into the tile to make a pattern, as a record of your walk. Carefully lift the tile out of the container and let it air dry.

BOGGARTS OR WOODLAND PUPPETS

Connie and a group of her friends were so inspired by the puppet in this photograph that they decided to invent some little people to live in the woods. They created all sorts of weird and wonderful puppets just from a heap of sticks and leaves, a few balls of clay and some natural paints.

This fearsome-looking creature is in fact a boggart: a malicious, unhelpful spirit who loves to cause havoc in the woods and play tricks on unwary passers-by. Forest School worker Kate Cheng makes boggarts with school parties, using them to pass on messages about the natural world. To make a boggart like Kate's, tie two sticks together with raffia or wool to make the body and arms. Add a well-worked ball of soft clay to make the head, moulding it to make features. Decorate with leaves and other natural materials; the leaves of this headdress were dipped in natural chalk paint (see page 115). Dress your boggart in a leafy outfit. It was the final addition of eyes made from yellow leaves and chalk paste that brought this wicked spirit alive.

MAROTTE PUPPETS

Marotte puppets evolved from the jester's stick, a wand topped with a head that was an integral part of a jester's performance. We made simple marotte puppets with a ball of clay and a stick, adding details with berries, feathers, leaves, chalk paint, flakes from a fir cone and maple seeds. How fierce can you make your puppet?

DECORATIVE CLAY TILES

Some years ago our local primary school embarked on a project to make a three-dimensional mural of clay tiles. Each class contributed to a panel depicting a different aspect of school life. It was a wonderful way to involve everyone in a communal art project.

To make your own three-dimensional tiles:

● Find two pieces of wooden baton about 1cm/1/2in thick and at least 30cm/12in long.

● Place them in parallel and about 15cm/6in apart on an old piece of sheet laid on a flat surface. Then roll out the clay between them to an even thickness.

● Cut out a square tile from the clay and allow it to become leather hard.

● The fun comes in decorating the tile by scratching the surface or roughening an area, and then using slip to stick on three-dimensional details made in moulded clay. If you wish, draw out a design for your tile and cut out pieces of the design to use as templates to cut around to make your 3-D clay details.

● Try rolling clay over textured fabrics such as hessian or old lace and then cutting out the textured pieces to stick on to your tile. Clay pushed through an old sieve makes excellent trees or hedges or even woolly sheep. Stick all the pieces down very carefully so that no air is trapped underneath them.

● Fired tiles can be painted with model paints. A tile is only decorative, so doesn't need to be glazed.

Safety tips

● **Never collect clay near polluted water courses or from contaminated land.**

● **Always wash hands well after working with clay.**

PLASTER OF PARIS TILES

Raw clay can be used to make textured tile moulds imprinted with images of natural objects. From these you can make quick-setting plaster of Paris tiles.

You will need

- Natural clay
- Small plastic containers
- Natural objects such as shells, cones, leaves with prominent veins – anything that might leave a three-dimensional imprint when pushed into clay
- Plaster of Paris, water and a stick for mixing
- String
- An old toothbrush and a cocktail stick

MAKING THE TILES

- Flatten well-worked clay into a plastic tray to make a smooth layer at least 1.5cm/3/4in deep. Leave it to dry a little while you collect some natural materials.
- Press the objects into the clay to make imprints.
- Sprinkle plaster of Paris into a container of water, mixing it with a stick until it reaches the consistency of porridge. Don't let it get too thick. Pour the prepared plaster of Paris over the clay mould to a thickness of at least 1.5cm/1/4in.
- Use a stick to push a loop of string into the top of the plaster so that you can hang the finished tile up.
- When the plaster has set hard, turn the plastic container upside down and press to push the clay and plaster of Paris out.
- Separate the clay and plaster. Clean the tile with a toothbrush and cocktail stick. When it has dried completely, paint and varnish it.

Safety tip

- **Plaster of Paris becomes very hot when mixed with water: do not let anyone put their fingers or anything else into the liquid plaster and always use a stick or spoon for mixing.**

PINCH POTS

One of the simplest ways of working with clay, this gives a real feel for the way it behaves.

- Roll clay between your palms to make a smooth sphere about the size of a tennis ball.
- Push your thumb into the centre to create a well.
- Slowly pinch up the walls of the pot, turning it constantly in one hand while pinching it between the fingers and thumb of the other hand to keep an even thickness. Don't rush at it but work slowly, doing just a little at a time and building up a regular rhythm of pinching and turning, pinching and turning. The walls of the finished pot should be approximately 6mm/1/3 in.
- Gently pat the bottom of the pot on to a smooth surface to make a flat base.

- Be careful not to let the rim become thin and cracked.
- Smooth the surface of the pot with a little water on your hands, to remove cracks and create a smooth finish.
- If you wish, decorate the pot by pressing natural objects such as conker cases, shells, cones, leaves or hollow twigs into the soft clay.
- Cover the pot lightly in plastic and leave for a day or two so that it dries out a little to become 'leather hard'. This makes it easier to scratch intricate patterns into the surface with a blackthorn pin or a twig: the clay will cut cleanly without sticking to the cutting tool.
- Rubbing an old spoon over the surface of the leather-hard pot using a circular motion will create a smoother shiny surface.
- Leave the pots out to air dry before firing.

SCULPTURES

A few years ago Hannah and Lily spent an afternoon with Carol making clay sculptures that were later fired in a kiln. We still have a delightful clay chicken in pride of place in our garden. Its hollow, smooth design made it easy to fire.

Sculptures for firing must have very strong joints that are thoroughly attached to the body of the piece. To fix joints securely, scratch both surfaces and then brush them with slip (watered-down clay which can be used as glue). To save ruining a paintbrush, use an old toothbrush both to roughen up the surface and to apply the slip.

POTS AND SCULPTURES FOR FIRING

Everyone was keen to make pots and fire them, but we knew we would have to be careful to avoid the pots exploding in the high temperatures. If pockets of air or water are trapped in the clay, these expand on heating, causing an explosion.

To minimize the risk of this happening, knead the clay so that you expel the air: push it down into a wedge shape and rotate it, squeezing and pushing. Avoid folding, as this traps air. Any thick clay should be hollowed out. Make sure that walls are not overly thick and that all joints are thoroughly worked and smooth. Let pots, sculptures and tiles dry out completely over a period of two to three weeks before firing; they are dry enough when they stop changing colour.

FIRING CLAY

If clay is heated to at least 700°C its chemical composition changes and the separate particles bind together. This is the point at which clay turns into 'pottery' and the process becomes irreversible.

It must have been such a revelation when people first discovered that soft clay could be transformed into a hard, durable and stable material suitable for a wide range of uses.

There is no need to fire clay in an expensive kiln: more accessible methods include using fire in a simple pit, in an improvised brick kiln or in a galvanized incinerator bin.

Pit fire kiln

A pit fire is more effective than an open fire because the heat surrounds the pots. First warm the pots by placing them near the fire. Then transfer them into the pit and cover them with more sticks and perhaps sawdust. Cover the pit with an old tin sheet and leave the fire to cool as slowly as possible to minimize breakages. Only remove the pots when it is quite cold.

Brick kiln

If you have access to some old bricks, build a square structure as illustrated. Put the pots into this kiln on top of a layer of sawdust, cover with more sawdust and then make your fire on top of that. Cover the whole thing with a metal sheet or metal dustbin lid and leave the fire to burn itself out. Remove the pots when the kiln has cooled.

Firing in an incinerator bin

We decided to fire our pinch pots in an incinerator bin with ventilation holes and a chimney lid (available from gardening and DIY stores), placing the bin on paving slabs in a garden.

● The pots must be very hot when you place them in your improvised kiln. On the day of firing, we put the prepared dried pots in a cold oven and heated it up to its highest temperature.

● While the pots are in the oven, make a fire in your bin. We used kindling to get the fire going quickly to a high temperature and build up a good base of ash; then we piled larger pieces of dry wood on top and waited for it to really get going.

● Using thermal mittens and metal tongs, place the pots gently into the bin. Our pots immediately started changing from brown to black in colour. We placed dry leaves over the pots, then put the lid on the bin and let it burn itself out. You could use sawdust to cover the pots instead of leaves.

● Alternatively, you could bury your cold pots in sawdust in the bottom of a cold bin and then build the fire on top. Once the fire is raging, put the lid on. The pots will heat up gradually as the temperature rises.

● Once the bin has cooled completely, open the lid and remove any ashes to reveal your fired pots. Don't be disappointed if some have cracked in the intense heat – even the best potters expect to lose a few.

SMOKE DECORATING

Clay is usually glazed after firing, but we wanted to find a more natural method of decoration. Our friend Jane White has explored the ancient art of smoke firing, in which you heat previously fired clay wrapped in or covered with organic materials such as leaves to create vibrant designs and colours reminiscent of natural patterns in stones, bark or even clouds.

They are placed in a pit or a brick kiln, where the combination of fire and the chemicals released from the organic materials transforms the clay's surface. Exposed clay is coloured dark by the smoke, but any covered areas are protected and may pick up colours or shapes.

Smoke firing is quite an ambitious project, and should always be carefully supervised by adults. You need to be prepared to take risks and learn by trial and error – it's impossible to predict how each pot will come out.

What you need

Smoke firing works best on pale-coloured pots, so the dark pots made in your home-made kiln may give disappointing results. We found some pale-coloured and in-expensive unglazed pot bases in a garden centre. Try smoke decorating with some of the following materials:

- **Dried organic materials**: Jane has experimented with skins of pineapple, citrus fruit, bananas and onions, and with nutshells, seaweed, grasses and leaves. Dry organic materials thoroughly in a warm oven before using them.
- **Salted rags or string**: soak these in a strong salt solution for a few days and then wrap around the pots. Or try seaweed or leaves soaked in salt and then dried – the trace elements in salt can produce unique colours.
- **Slip (watered-down clay)**: Paint this on the pots, and then let it dry and scratch patterns in the slip. Make sure the pots are thoroughly dry before firing. After smoke firing, wash off the slip – you may need to use a scouring pad.

Smoking the clay

- Wrap fired clay pots in whatever materials you wish to use. Or, if using slip, paint it on to the pots, let it dry and scratch patterns into it. Remember that the smoke won't colour those areas covered by slip.
- Place a thick layer of sawdust in a metal rubbish bin, a brick kiln or a fire pit, and put the prepared pots on top. Cover the pots in more sawdust and then build a fire over the top. Set it alight, cover and leave to burn.
- We also had a go at just burning scrunched-up newspaper in a metal rubbish bin instead of making a fire. This works quite effectively but won't reach such high temperatures as a wood fire, and you may need to fill the bin with paper more than once. If using this quick-firing method, you could use masking tape to make a pattern, or melted candle wax applied with an old brush.

- Remove your pots once the kiln has cooled down completely. Prepare to be disappointed or amazed!
- Polish the pots with a little beeswax to produce a sheen and enrich the colours.

Safety tips

- **Always seek adult supervision when working with fire.**
- **The temperatures required to fire clay are very intense, so once the pots are in the improvised kiln, don't remove them until everything has completely cooled.**
- **Smoke-fired pots are for decorative purposes only, as they remain porous. See the fire safety tips on page 156.**

MAKE IT
FROM WOOD

RUSTIC FURNITURE

DRIFTWOOD SCULPTURES

TWIG SCULPTURE

WILD BASKETS

WITHY LANTERNS

MAKE IT FROM WOOD

We weren't convinced that the workshop would go down well at all and wondered how they could possibly make a basket in just an hour and a half. About twelve young people arrived at the appointed time, kicking off their shoes before bending down to enter the cave-like yurt. While their eyes adjusted to the dim light, they sat in a circle around basket maker Amanda of Wyldwood Willow. As she showed them her baskets, they began to look a little daunted – how on earth were they going to be able to do this?

But as they followed Amanda's clear step-by-step instructions the atmosphere changed to one of quiet yet companionable concentration. This was no quick fix: basket making needs time, dexterity and co-ordination. But the workshop flew by far too quickly and everyone succeeded in making their own willow basket to take home and treasure. Easily available, versatile and renewable, wood in all its forms used to be the commonest and most inexpensive material for many household and garden items. Many of today's so-called wild woodlands were managed and shaped over hundreds of years for a range of wood products. In recent years there has been something of a revival in woodland crafts, but it is perhaps the growth in popularity of willow weaving that has been most dramatic. This versatile and easily worked material can be used to create almost anything you wish.

Wood has always appealed to children. Green wood can be whittled to make a pea-shooter or carved into a bow and arrow. Generations of young people have used wood to enhance their games or make their own toys. This chapter includes a few ideas for weaving, whittling, carving and sculpting. There are smaller projects suitable for individuals and more ambitious projects suitable for a team working together. Several of these activities involve using knives and other tools and should only be carried out under adult supervision.

RUSTIC FURNITURE

We thought the course on making rustic garden chairs in the woods would probably involve using large dangerous tools, so it might appeal to our fifteen-year-old sons. But of course, when the day arrived they weren't at all keen on the idea. It was the middle of their precious summer holidays and if we hadn't been photographing for this book we would probably have gone for an easy life and let them stay in bed. However, after a very slow start they threw themselves into the task in hand and by the end of an absorbing day they had produced two distinctive chairs.

Making these chairs requires some competence in dealing with sharp tools; this isn't an activity for young children. Freshly cut green wood is better than older wood, as it's less likely to split when nailed.

Rustic furniture is eco-friendly and cheap, but don't expect it to last all that long. Each piece will be different, and you could be really creative and incorporate quirky design features. Have a go too at making other pieces of rustic furniture. For example, join together a series of straight thin logs by binding with rope or nailing into place, and then add some legs to make a raft-type bench or table.

You will need
- 2 long back legs (approximately 1–1.5m/3–5ft × 7cm/3in)
- 2 short front legs (approximately 45cm/18in × 7cm/3in)
- 8 rungs (approximately 45cm/18in × 5cm/2in)
- A variety of thinner branches for the seat, back and arms
- 30–40 long nails, minimum 7cm/3in (depending on the thickness of your wood)
- Loppers, bow saw, hammer and some imagination!

MAKING THE CHAIR

● Place the two long back legs on the ground parallel to each other and about 35cm/14in apart. Join the legs together by nailing a rung at the height you want the seat. Nail another one below this to form a square.

● Place the two short front legs on the ground parallel to each other and join with two rungs as above. Make sure the rungs are at the same height on both pairs of legs.

Stand the front and back legs beside each other on level ground and ask someone to hold them so that you can keep everything parallel. Nail rungs on to each side to make the basic structure of your chair.

To increase strength, add two cross pieces on to each side.

Add branches for the seat and back. There are many different ways of doing this – make up your own design. Edward added arms to his chair and Jake found some lovely shaped twigs, making more of a throne.

To help your chair last longer and look better, paint it with a mixture of 50 per cent white spirit and 50 per cent linseed oil.

Sit down gingerly and see if your chair survives!

Safety tips

This activity is quite complex and requires the use of large tools – it should be closely supervised by adults.

Be aware of tool safety: see page 156.

DRIFTWOOD SCULPTURES

Dan was intrigued by the shapes of the driftwood he found on a Cornish beach. He investigated each piece, turning them round in his hands, looking for possibilities. He began to see that it would take only a little work to transform one piece of driftwood into a goose. He found a piece for a body and took his finds back to the holiday cottage, where he fixed them together with screws and used a drill to make holes for the feet. He was on a roll now – and before long he had transformed other pieces into a seal and a pig.

Moulded by the relentless pounding of waves and bleached by the sun, driftwood has been shaped by natural forces. Perhaps it has come from the other side of the world; perhaps it has been tossed about in the sea for years before we stumble across it on a beach. When visiting the coast, search along the shoreline for naturally sculpted wood, and have a go at bringing out the shapes hidden within. Perhaps the marks in the grain suggest a face; or a smooth stick might resemble a limb. Use your imagination: can you see an animal, a bird or a boat? Other gathered materials might enhance the sculpture – perhaps some shell eyes or seaweed hair. Make an ephemeral sculpture to leave behind at the beach, or take a few bits of wood home to fix together with nails or glue.

TWIG SCULPTURE

Blending traditional basketry skills with a freer, more random approach to weaving, this is something anyone can do. There are a few basic pointers and the rest is up to you, as our teenage sons found out when they had a go. Although any bendy twigs can be used, willow is perhaps the most suitable because it is particularly flexible. Use it for weaving any sculptural form, from animals and birds to flowing shapes and architectural structures.

We attended a workshop run by willow weaver David Gosling. We used 2m/6ft dried willow rods soaked in water. Freshly cut willow, hazel or other pliable twigs are also suitable, but make sure you weave them as tightly as you can, because fresh materials will shrink as they dry.

Always use very bendy twigs – they have to put up with lots of pushing and squashing into shape. The only other thing you need is a pair of secateurs. Willow sculptures will last for only a couple of years unless you coat them in wood preservative.

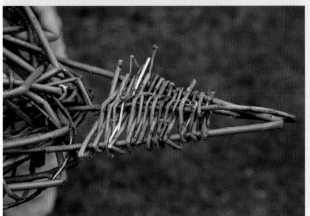

WILLOW SCULPTING BASICS

- **A sphere:** The basic building block. Make a circle from one length of willow by bending it around and then weaving the ends up and around each other until they are fixed in place. Make two more circles the same size. Then push one circle inside another one at right angles and pull the third one over the top to produce a basic sphere. This can be squashed into an oval – perhaps the start of an animal's body. Or fill in the gaps by adding more willow circles to make a more complete ball.
- **Plaiting:** Push three or four willow rods into the ground and plait them together.
- **Binding:** Hold several rods together in one hand, and then wind another rod around and around them to bind them together. Make

the binding tight and neat, and thread the end down through the middle to complete.
- **Weaving:** We made this goose tail by taking three short straight thick lengths of willow, holding them at an angle and then weaving thinner willow up and around them. The supports should be about twice the thickness of the weaving rods.

Safety tip
- **Use secateurs with care.**

WILD BASKETS

This might seem a little ambitious, but we saw for ourselves how a group of young people can make baskets in just an hour and a half. They worked with commercially grown dried willow (you can find suppliers on the internet), which had been soaked before using. But they could have used any long narrow plant material that passes the wrist test – that is, it can be wound around your wrist without snapping.

Many hedgerows, woodland and garden plants are suitable for basketry, from climbers such as ivy, clematis, Virginia creeper and honeysuckle to trees and shrubs such as hazel, dogwood, birch, broom and eucalyptus. Recycle all those autumn and winter prunings by transforming them into traditional baskets or random weave sculptures, making the most of different textures and colours. If using fresh materials, weave very tightly to allow for shrinkage or leave them in a damp shady spot for a few weeks to shrink a little; if they become too dry, soak for a week to soften them, as otherwise they will crack.

What you need

- 6 rods of willow or some other bendy wood, all the same length (these will be your structural rods) – about 1.3m/4ft long, with no side branches or injuries
- Many weaving rods (or weavers), thinner than the structural rods
- Bradawl, screw driver or metal skewer and secateurs

GETTING STARTED

These instructions are for a right-handed weaver.

- Take the three thickest structural rods and push the bradawl gently through the centre of each. Wiggle it from side to side, tearing the fibres to make a slit. Use a finger to ease them a little further apart. Line the three rods up in parallel, thick end to thin end.
- Thread the other structural rods through the slits, making a cross as shown. These rods also need to be thick end to thin end: as you make the basket you will spread them out like spokes, and it will look better if it has an even shape.
- Lay your cross down on the ground to find its natural curve before deciding which way up to make your basket. Gently press the cross over your knee to enhance the curve. Always work on your basket this way up – that is, with the bottom of the basket facing you.
- Work with the basket on your knees, bracing it against your tummy. If you're right-handed, weave from the left-hand side of the basket (let's call it the west) up towards the structural rods facing furthest way from you (the north). Or think of the whole thing as a clock face, and work at the two o'clock position.

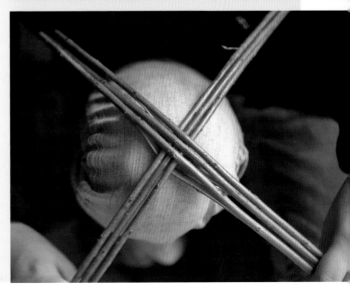

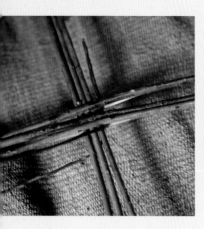

To start with, the split structural rods need to be in the east–west position. Take two weavers of equal thickness and length and insert their tips into the slits to the left of the north–south-facing structural rods as shown. Now you are ready to start weaving.

Take one weaver (A) around in front of three structural rods and the other (B) behind. Then cross them over so that weaver A goes behind the next three structural rods and weaver B goes in front of them. Keep weaving like this in a clockwise direction until you have two rows of weaving all the way round. Turn the cross as you weave so that you're always working at that two o'clock position.

The next stage is to splay out the structural rods. Look at the three structural rods facing north, and gently pull the left-hand rod down towards the left. Weave over and under it and then over and under the central rod. When you get to the right-hand north structural rod, pull it gently down to the right and then weave over and under it. Now turn the whole basket and do the same to the rest of the structural rods, until you have a star shape with an even spread.

Keep turning the basket in the same direction as you work, with your hands weaving as close as possible to the centre. Use your left hand like a vice, keeping the weave as tight as you can. Every so often push the basket gently down over your knee to increase the curve.

Get the pattern into your brain and just keep repeating it over and over again. It should become quite automatic after a while.

As you reach the end of your first weaver, choose two new weavers of a similar size. This time, start with the thick ends and simply poke them in alongside the ends of the old weavers and continue weaving; the new weavers will soon be fixed in place.

Whenever you start new weavers, join thin end to thin end and thick end to thick end.

Finishing off

Always finish off at the thin end of the weavers.

Weave the last ends in and out like a running stitch.

Use secateurs to snip off the ends as neatly as you can. Cut them at an angle so that they are flush with the basket's shape, and as short as you can make them.

WITHY LANTERNS

His art exam was looming ever closer and still Jake hadn't been inspired. Then he remembered making withy lanterns on a camping trip and he wondered if he could develop that idea.

After sticking a few lengths of bendy willow into the ground, he sculpted some large random shapes. Next he coated each piece of willow in diluted PVA glue before carefully placing tissue paper over the top and pulling it tightly across the frame. Then he sponged more PVA over the tissue and added further tissue layers. Once it was dry he decorated the tissue with paintings and drawings. The final piece looked very dramatic – the perfect way to light a marquee for a celebratory party as well as meeting the exam brief!

It was a visiting artist at Dan's school who first inspired us to make withy lanterns. She worked with groups of children to make giant brightly coloured shapes that had a beautiful translucent quality when lit. Withy lanterns are popular at festivals and celebrations; sometimes artists work with local communities to create huge lanterns to mark special occasions. Use these during a picnic or an outdoor meal in the garden. Or put each lantern on a long pole and have a procession, perhaps making it part of some outdoor theatre or storytelling.

You will need

- Thin bendy twigs stripped of leaves
  – we used hazel and willow
- Masking tape and PVA glue,
  old paintbrushes and sponges
- Coloured tissue paper (or try using
  hand-made paper – see pages 134–9)
- Night lights and small jars
- Scissors and secateurs

MAKING THE LANTERNS

- Fix some twigs together with masking tape to make a base of whatever shape you wish. Using more twigs, build up from the base to make a frame. Add a loop at the top so you will be able to hang up the lantern or carry it on a stick.
- Secure a small jar on to the base of the lantern with tape.
- Fix the tissue paper in place with tape or by painting diluted PVA on to the twigs and then placing the paper over the top. Sponging PVA on the tissue paper makes it much stronger and also gives it a translucent quality, but you need to allow time for it to dry. Add different colours of paper if you wish.
- Leave the base open so you can insert the night light into the jar and light it. Cut a small hole at the top of the lantern to let the heat out.
- Hang your lantern in a chosen spot and light it carefully.

Safety tips

- **Do not use sharp tools unless adults are around.**
- **Attach the jars securely to the lantern's base and make sure the night lights are not in contact with the tissue paper.**
- **Never leave the lanterns unattended.**

NATURE'S PIGMENTS

NATURAL PAINTS

NATURAL DYES

NATURE'S PIGMENTS

The milky blue of glacial melt water, the rainbow iridescence of a starling's plumage, the purple of an angry sky, the yellow splodge of lichen on a rock – the natural world is awash with colour. Some colours cry out at you, such as the unbelievable turquoise of a shallow sea or a poppy field's scarlet blaze.

Others are more hidden, like the hazel's minuscule red female flowers or the blue flash on a jay's wing, or subtler, like the multitudes of greens in a meadow. And some shades gain strength from their place in nature: I remember collecting wonderful coloured pebbles at the beach, only to find that their magic had faded by the time I got them home, away from the sea-washed shore.

With a little coaxing many natural materials release colours we can use as paints or even dyes. One of Hannah's art assignments was to use non-conventional paint to create a still-life picture of a pile of random objects. She gathered fruits and leaves from the garden, then crushed and strained them to create her own paint palette – purple from blackberries, red from damsons, green from parsley and brown from mint. Although she wasn't totally satisfied with the picture, she enjoyed experimenting with new media.

Early artists – such as those who made the cave paintings at Lascaux in France and Altamira in Spain – used whatever colours were available in their local environment. They ground up charcoal, ochre and haematite, probably mixing them to a paste with saliva, to produce a range of colours from black and brown through to reds and yellows. And perhaps the first dyers were inspired to add colours to their daily lives after noticing how berries left red stains on their fingers. Right up until the nineteenth century every dye came directly from natural sources, including plants (leaves, flowers, berries, stems or roots), insects, shellfish and minerals. This chapter includes some simple suggestions for experimenting with plants and minerals to make your own natural paints and dyes.

NATURAL PAINTS

One afternoon in the school holidays we met up in the woods to see what natural paints we could make. After collecting some likely-looking plant and mineral materials, everyone began pounding, grinding, mixing, straining – doing whatever they had to do to release colour.

What you need

- Plant and mineral materials such as soil, chalk, ash, leaves, berries and nuts – see what you can find and then experiment
- A pestle and mortar, and an old sieve or tea strainer (no longer used for cooking)
- Plastic containers and paintbrushes

COLOURS TO MAKE

● **WHITE:** Grind chalk into a powder, and mix with a little water to the consistency of double cream.

● **BLACK:** Use burnt wood, ash or charcoal. We mixed ash from the fireplace with water.

● **PURPLE AND RED:** Pick berries such as elderberries, blackberries, raspberries and rose hips. Squeeze through a sieve to make a purée; add water if needed.

● **BROWN:** Try collecting mud and clay in different locations – the colour may range from deep brown to a rich red. Rotting wood or bark should also release a brown colour.

● **RED/BROWN:** We crushed up old brick to make a red-brown colour. A bit of a cheat, but at least it was originally made from clay!

● **GREEN:** Pound grass and leaves with the pestle and mortar to release the green-tinged sap. If the green isn't strong enough, try boiling leaves with a little water to enhance the shade.

Mix your natural paints together to see what other shades you can make. Then use them to paint pictures on paper, wood, bark, stones or leaves. For a real Stone Age experience, use feathers, moss or even dried grass instead of an ordinary paintbrush. Or make your own primitive paintbrush by chewing on one end of a non-toxic twig to separate the fibres.

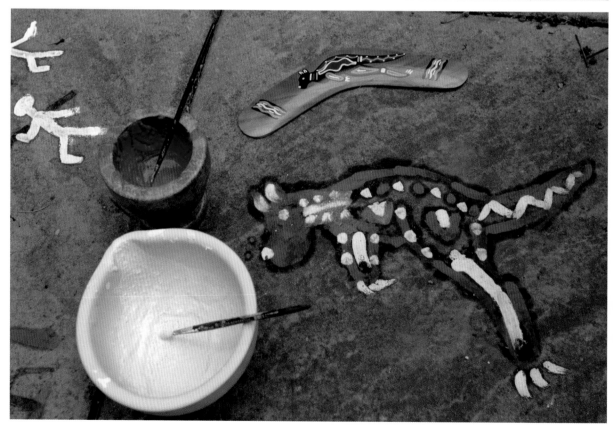

INSPIRED BY ABORIGINAL PAINTINGS

After an Australian visitor had shown us some amazing Aboriginal art, the children wanted to find out more. They discovered that traditional Aboriginal art is a complex means of communication – storytelling through pictures. They noticed how the designs often featured marsupials, lizards and snakes as well as complex patterns and swirls made up of lines and dots. Aboriginals used paintings to decorate rock, wood, bark, and even their own bodies. They applied paint with hands, with stringy bark or pliant twigs and with brushes made from hair. These were perfect ways to use our natural colours and we painted rocks, pebbles, wood, bark and even paving slabs. A kangaroo on a decorated boomerang inspired Connie, while Hannah painted a frog, Agnes a spooky face, and others made all sorts of swirling patterns and designs. Two girls copied the patterns on some highly coloured, stripy snails they found.

If you wish to keep any outdoor paintings, make sure you do them on something loose such as bark or a pebble. If painting on a fixed object, such as a rock or a tree trunk, either do it in a tucked-away place out of sight or wash it off once you have photographed it. This activity can be done anywhere, whether out on an expedition or in the back garden.

CHALK PAINT PATTERNS

If you are in an area where the local rock is chalk, look for lumps of it among upturned tree roots or exposed banks, wash it and make a chalky paste, as described on page 115. We put some in a bottle and took it on a walk. Someone started fiddling around, dipping sticks into the paste and arranging them into a star shape. Since then we have used our chalk paint in many settings, making patterns in unexpected places or using it to make little decorations. We have used it as a homemade face and body paint; inspired by pictures of Aboriginal body painting, the children have covered their faces, hands, arms and bodies in elaborate and scary designs. We have also used it along with clay slip and mud to coat stones and sticks to be left as a trail.

NATURAL DYES

Connie and Sophie had a wonderful messy time squashing and straining elderberries and were convinced that the vivid purple liquid would be perfect for tie dying.

They found a couple of old vests, tied them tightly with elastic bands and left them to soak in heated elderberry juice. After rinsing the vests in cold water to remove excess colour, they tore off the elastic bands to reveal spectacular patterns on a purple background. But the next day they were bitterly disappointed to find that the vibrant colour had faded to a horrible dirty grey. Clearly this activity needed a bit more research!

We collected blackberries, bark, acorns, bracken and dock and the children had much fun crushing, chopping and mixing. The bracken produced a lovely bright green when

ground with a pestle and mortar and mixed with a little water, and Connie spent ages chopping acorns into tiny pieces. We boiled each material and then simmered them for an hour or so. We tested the colours out on pieces of muslin – purple from the blackberries and beige from the acorns. But the colours weren't vibrant, so we still weren't satisfied. We knew that many dyes can be made from plants, so, not wanting to repeat the elderberry experience, we attended an inspirational natural dying workshop run by Jenny Dean. Finally we discovered a few simple ways to produce vibrant, non-fading shades that reflect the colours of the natural world.

A FEW TIPS ON NATURAL DYEING

Natural dyestuffs

Many common plants produce dyes, but some require the addition of another substance, known as a mordant, to bind the colour to the fabric. To keep things simple, we recommend choosing dyes that don't need a mordant. These are known as substantive dyes, and sources could include:

- **Trees:** Birch bark (pink), alder bark or cones (green), eucalyptus leaves and bark (rust and orange), walnut leaves (olive green) and ripe nut husks (brown), ripe oak acorns and galls (grey and brown – the acorns need to be chopped finely and soaked for several days before simmering). Only remove bark from trees that have been cut down or are dead.
- **Other plants:** Rhubarb root (yellow), comfrey leaves (green), blackberry leaves and shoots (green) and ripe berries (blue – but you need to simmer berries for half an hour and then strain and heat the fabric in the dye bath before steeping overnight), madder (red).
- **Kitchen spices:** Try using turmeric, which produces olive-green shades.

Materials for dyeing

We experimented on lengths of wool, silk and cotton and found that wool consistently absorbed more colour. Try to use 100 per cent natural fibres; manmade fibres like nylon don't absorb colour so readily. Always weigh the fibres or fabric beforehand so that you can calculate how much dyestuff to use (the rule of thumb is half the weight of dyestuff to fabric). And you don't have to stick to fabrics – have a go at dyeing other natural materials such as wood, shells or stones, stems of willow, leaves you plan to weave with or even paper.

Colour modifiers

This was a revelation to us! Certain substances, including various everyday materials, modify colours on fibres after they have been dyed, so you can produce several colours from just one dyestuff. Either add modifiers to a used dye bath or put them in a separate bowl of water.

- **Acidic modifier:** Use about half a cupful of clear vinegar or lemon juice in a 1-litre/2-pint bowl of water.

- **Alkaline modifiers:** Add 2 tablespoons of washing soda dissolved in a cupful of boiling water to about 1 litre/2 pints of water. Or make wood-ash water by putting cold wood ashes from a fireplace to soak in a bucket of water for a week or so, and then gently pour off the water without disturbing the sediment.

- **Iron modifier:** Soak rusty nails or an old horseshoe in a bucket of vinegar and water for a couple of weeks. Pour off the liquid to use as a modifier.

- **Copper modifier:** Soak a length of old copper pipe in a bucket of vinegar and water for a week or so. Pour off the liquid to use as a modifier.

The dyeing process

We tried dyeing with rhubarb root, testing it on cotton, silk and wool. You too may wish to start out by testing small amounts of fabric until you discover which colours you like and which dyestuffs work best for you. Natural dyeing involves a lot of trial and error – just have a go and see what colours you can conjure up. This is quite a messy activity, best done outside using a camping stove or fire.

What you need

- Dyestuffs, modifiers and fabric
- Pestle and mortar (not used for cooking)
- Weighing scales
- Selection of stainless-steel, enamelled or glass heatproof bowls or saucepans (no longer used for cooking); all implements must be non-reactive, so don't use brass, copper or iron
- Fabric to be dyed – only use clean natural fabric
- Plastic buckets
- Wire-mesh strainer or sieve
- Old apron or old shirt to cover your clothes, and rubber gloves
- Old wooden spoons, or better still some sticks, for stirring with – separate ones for each dyestuff and each modifier

Preparing the dye

- Bruise or crush the dyestuff thoroughly. The larger the surface area of the dyestuff, the more colour the fabric will be exposed to. Crush with a stone, or in an old pestle and mortar. We used dried rhubarb root, chopped up into small pieces; if using fresh rhubarb root, putting it in the deep freeze helps break down the tough fibres.
- Weigh out the dyestuff – about half the weight of the fabric.
- Put the prepared dyestuff in a bowl and add boiling water.
- Leave overnight. If the colour isn't strong enough, bring the mixture to the boil and simmer for a while.
- Leave to cool and then strain the liquid into an old metal bowl. This will be your dye bath.

Prepare your fabric

- Put a splash of washing-up liquid in a bowl or bucket of water, and then rinse the fabric that is to be dyed until all the fibres are soaked.
- Squeeze the fabric to remove excess water.

Dyeing the fabric

- Place the wet fabric in the dye bath, adding more water if need be.
- Place the pan over a fire or stove and raise the temperature gradually. Simmer for 30–45 minutes and then leave to cool, preferably overnight.
- Remove the fabric from the dye pan. In our case the rhubarb had dyed the fabric an orangey-yellow shade.
- Some dyes work better if left to soak for a day or two.

Modifying

If you would like to experiment further, try using modifiers. Place the dyed fabric into a bowl of modifier, or add the modifier to the used dye bath and soak the dyed fabric in that. Begin by using a small amount of modifying solution, adding more if you wish to enhance the colour change. Keep different modifiers separate to avoid cross-contamination.

We used the four modifiers described above to produce the following colours on our rhubarb-dyed fabrics, as illustrated in the photograph opposite, clockwise from the top:

- **Iron solution** – grey-green shade
- **Copper solution** – rusty shade
- **Clear vinegar solution** – bright yellow wool and creamy yellow cotton
- **Washing soda solution** – pink shade

Finishing

Add a little pH-neutral washing-up liquid to a bucket of water. Then rinse the dyed fabric thoroughly before hanging it up to dry.

MAKE YOUR OWN TIE-DYE T-SHIRT

Connie made this spectacular tie-dye shirt in an indigo dye vat organized for us by Jenny Dean. Anyone wishing to use indigo should follow our example and join a dyeing course, but how about making your own multicoloured tie-dye T-shirt with just one natural dye and a couple of modifiers? For example, you could dye it yellow in a rhubarb dye, and then tie it with elastic bands before soaking in a modifier. You could then tie it up even more and put it in another modifier to produce a three-coloured tie-dye pattern.

Safety tips

- Don't collect rare or poisonous plants. Use a plant identification book or go out with someone who knows about plants, and only gather modest quantities of plant materials.
- Never use the same pots or tools for food preparation and dyeing.
- Store all dyes and modifiers in clearly labelled containers.
- Be careful when throwing away dyeing materials. Dilute all solutions before pouring them down the drain.
- Wear rubber gloves when handling dyes and modifiers.
- Be careful when working with hot pans.
- Some dyes can be harmful if ingested.
- When dyeing indoors, ensure that the room is well ventilated.
- See the fire safety tips on page 156.

NATURAL CRAFTS

JEWELLERY

PAPER MAKING

LEAF PLATES AND BOWLS

BULRUSH DOLLS

PEWTER CASTING

FELTING

MAKING A LEATHER PURSE

NATURAL MOBILES AND WINDCHIMES

NATURAL CRAFTS

On a trip to the fringes of the Kalahari Desert we were greeted by a group of San people eager to show us necklaces made of seeds and pods, hollow stems and intricately decorated nuts. We bought a few to take home, and these pieces of natural jewellery remind us of a remarkable people whose ancient way of life, so totally interdependent with nature, is increasingly threatened by the unreasonable demands of the modern world.

Aboriginal peoples have always had a deep understanding of and empathy with the natural world as well as a deep respect for its integrity. They have always known how to use it without abusing it, and how to gather and make all they need, from food and shelter to clothes and decorations, without jeopardizing their ability to continue to do so in the future. Before industrialization most communities throughout the world were pretty much self-sufficient, creating many of the practical and decorative things they needed from nature's resources, and passing traditional skills down through the generations. Nowadays if we want something we tend to want it right now, so we rush off to the shops and buy it. Yet working with natural materials to create useful and beautiful things can be a source of deep satisfaction and pleasure, as well providing a valuable link with our past.

This chapter is all about looking at natural materials in a new way – discovering the intrinsic beauty in a smooth pebble, a colourful feather or a piece of driftwood and spotting their potential to be transformed into something else. Each memento will have something of the essence of wildness – perhaps the hint of a smell, the feel of the sea's power or the memory of a special place. Always remember to harvest natural materials sustainably, leaving plenty behind for the future.

JEWELLERY

On a lonely windswept beach Hannah found a shell skeleton. It had been scarred, smoothed and shaped by the sea, and only an indication of its helix shape and its central post remained. It made a perfect souvenir pendant: she needs only to feel its cool smoothness to summon potent memories of a time and place that will always be special to her.

In London's Natural History Museum, there are two artificially pierced marine shells that have been dated at about 100,000 years old. Probably the oldest pieces of jewellery ever discovered, they provide remarkable evidence that human beings have been appreciating the aesthetic qualities of natural materials for many thousands of years. From ancient times adornments were created from stones, seeds, berries, shells, feathers, fibres, bark, wood, bones, teeth – all sorts of mineral, plant and animal materials.

Make your own collection of nature's gifts and transform them into jewellery – whether ephemeral daisy earrings that will last for only an afternoon or a stone pendant to treasure for ever.

You will need

- A collection of materials (e.g. small cones, elder twigs, seeds, leaves, shells, pebbles, sea-smoothed glass, feathers)
- Threads – try making your own from plant fibres (e.g. nettles, flax) or use linen thread, wool or fine leather cord
- Needles, wire, earring loops, pendant settings and some very strong glue
- A bradawl and/or a sail needle and possibly a drill and a vice, as you may need to drill holes through pieces of wood or hard seeds
- Natural paints (e.g. ground chalk, see page 115)
- A wood-burning engraver or pyrograph pen for decorating wood or bark (available on the internet)

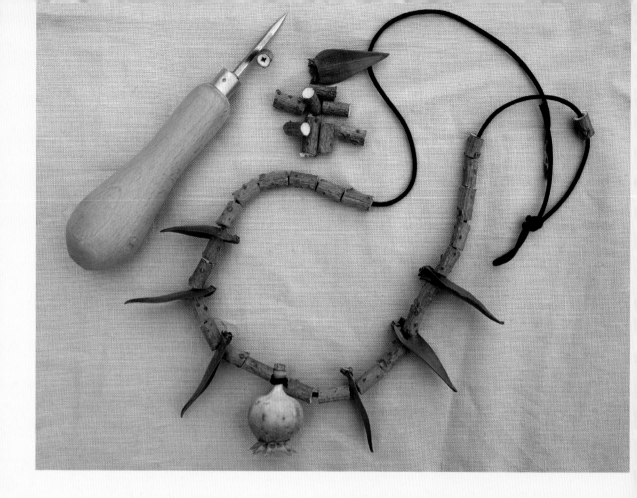

MAKING BEADS

All sorts of seeds, pods, nuts, flower petals and even leaves and stems can be made into beads. Softer seeds are easily threaded with wire or fibre. Drill holes through harder pods and nuts, or try soaking them in water to soften them so that you can get a needle through.

● **Rose hips:** The children of some North American tribes used to string rose hips on to threads to make necklaces. These look wonderful but won't last for long.

● **Corn grains:** The tribes of south-western Mexico make necklaces from different-coloured corn grains.

● **Elder stems:** The necklace above was made from elder stems cut into lengths and then hollowed out with a bradawl. These were threaded on to a cord, along with flakes from a cone and a poppy seed head. You could decorate the beads by burning marks on to the surface using a pyrograph pen, or painting with natural paints and then varnishing.

MAKING NECKLACES AND PENDANTS

To make a necklace or bracelet, thread beads on to a cord. You may wish to use all the same type of bead, or to mix and match, or to make a repeating pattern. Tie knots or add seeds, leaves or feathers between the beads to add interest.

Connie was inspired to make a pendant from a flake of Scots pine bark (the bark flakes off in interesting shapes with swirly brown and grey patterns). She stuck an honesty seed on to it, made a hole with a bradawl and threaded it on to some linen thread. She completed the pendant by making a nifty clasp from two acorn cups of different sizes, one fitting neatly into the other. She and her friend made another necklace from fir-cone flakes painted with a layer of chalk paint (see page 115). Once the paint had dried, they scratched a pattern into it with a bradawl or needle. They varnished the cone flakes with diluted PVA glue to preserve the pattern.

USING STONES AND SHELLS

Try making small stones, sea-smoothed glass or colourful shell fragments into simple pendants. All you need is a small metal setting with a flat area on which to stick the stone or glass and some very strong glue. Fix your chosen item on to the pendant setting with a good-sized dab of glue and leave to set before hanging from a ribbon, cord or a chain.

PAPER MAKING

I remember being intrigued by the paper birch tree during a trip to Canada as a young teenager, and I even wrote on the papery bark (a very short letter to my grandparents). But the most remarkable natural paper is that made by the oldest paper makers of all – wasps. They chew up weathered wood fibres with saliva to make a pulp, using their mouthparts and feet to spread it out into thin layers, from which they build their spherical nests.

The basic paper-making technique hasn't changed since the first true paper was made in China in about AD100. Much like the wasps' nest, it involves laying down a pulp of interlocking cellulose fibres and melding them together with friction and pressure. The first stage of the process involves making the pulp of plant tissues in water. During the second stage a mould is submerged into the pulp mixture and then lifted gently to the surface, trapping a thin layer of pulp in an even sheet as the water drains away.

Although the pulp is usually made of wood fibres, any fibrous vegetation as well as old paper is suitable, provided that the fibres are softened first. We had a wonderfully messy and rewarding session making paper from a variety of plant materials.

The mould and deckle

A mould is essential for creating a layer of pulp thin enough to become paper, and the deckle determines the shape of each sheet.

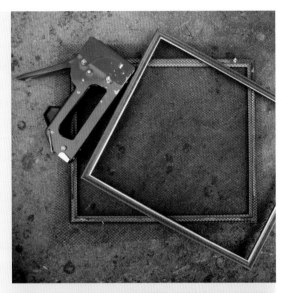

What you need

- Mesh. We found a fine plastic mesh (used for greenhouse shading) at a local garden centre. Other suitable meshes might include net curtains, mosquito netting, tapestry canvas or even a pair of old nylon tights
- Two old picture frames of the same size with the glass removed
- Staple gun or some tacks and a hammer

Making the mould and deckle

- Stretch the mesh tightly over one of the picture frames, fixing it in place with a staple gun. You could use drawing pins or tacks instead of a staple gun.
- The second picture frame (the deckle) should fit over the first. This helps to determine the paper's shape, size and thickness and stops pulp from spilling over the edge of the mould. If you prefer paper with irregular edges, don't use a deckle. We experimented with using different shapes as deckles and discovered that cookie and pastry cutters were ideal for making small paper shapes suitable for gift tags or coasters.

NATURAL PAPER

Suitable paper-making plants include reeds, bulrushes, sedges, blackberry (stems and leaves), iris leaves, willow stems, nettles and ferns. Harvest towards the end of the growing season when the fibres are strongest. Fruit and vegetable waste can also be used – try banana and citrus peel, onion skins or melon rinds. Or try using a combination of plant fibres with old paper blended to a pulp with some water.

What you need
● Plant materials, such as chopped-up stems and leaves
● Saucepans (not aluminium), metal spoons, metal sieve or colander, scissors and secateurs
● Some hardboard, cotton rags and a pile of newspapers
● Washing soda – an alkali to dissolve non-cellulose materials
● Bleach (we suggest using the more environmentally friendly chlorine-free bleach)
● Rubber gloves
● A large container of water, big enough to allow you to move the mould and deckle to and fro in the water
● Pre-pressed flowers, leaves or petals for extra decoration

MAKING THE PAPER

- Roughly chop the plant materials so they are small enough to fit into a large saucepan.
- Spread a rag over a piece of hardboard ready to receive your first piece of paper.
- Fill the pan about two-thirds full of the prepared plant materials and add water to cover. This will make about one sheet of A4 paper.
- Dissolve half a cup of washing soda in a cup of hot water and stir into the pan.
- Bring to the boil then simmer for 2–3 hours. Mix occasionally so that the material doesn't stick together in lumps. Add more water if necessary.
- Remove from the heat and leave to cool. Pour into a sieve or colander and rinse gently in cold water until the water runs clear; this removes non-cellulose material.
- Pour water into a 1-litre/2-pint bowl with about a quarter of a cup of bleach. Add the prepared plant materials and stir with a metal spoon. Leave to soak until the colour changes to yellow or cream; the longer you leave it, the paler it will be. The bleach can be used for several successive batches.
- Pour the pulp into a sieve or colander and rinse carefully to remove the bleach.
- Place the mould and deckle in the large container of water. The side of the mould with the mesh flush over the picture frame must face upwards so that it will be easy to remove the paper.
- Place the pulp on the mould. The netting of the mould should be submerged just below the water's surface so that the pulp moves around easily, ensuring an even spread. Add a little more pulp if the paper looks too thin.
- If you wish to add decoration, now is the moment to arrange some dried flowers, petals, or leaves on the pulp.
- When you are happy with the thickness and distribution of the pulp, gently lift the mould and deckle out of the water, holding them level.
- Remove the deckle and let the water drain off the mould. Rest one edge of the mould on the prepared cotton rag and hardboard, and in one rapid movement, tip the mould right over and then lift it carefully away. The paper should be left behind flat on the rag.
- Cover with another rag and then a wad of newspaper. Place a rag on top of the newspaper, ready for your next sheet of paper. When you've made your last piece of paper, place more newspaper on top and then some heavy books.
- Leave for a couple of days and then carefully pick up your flattened sheets of paper and hang them up to dry.

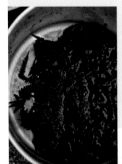

NETTLE PAPER

Nettles make very good paper, but before the bleaching stage you need to split the stems and scrape the inner threads away from the coarse outer layer, using a fingernail. Discard the outer layer – it is the inner layers and the leaves that make the smooth pulp. We made a series of nettle paper shapes.

Safety tips

- Limit your plant gathering to common species and don't disturb plant roots.
- Limit the use of bleach, dispose of it responsibly and wear rubber gloves when handling.
- This activity requires adult supervision, particularly when boiling plant materials and using bleach.

OAK AND CHESTNUT LEAVES

We found that prepared oak and chestnut leaves wouldn't blend together as a sheet but could be mixed with plant or paper pulp to make paper. The leaves became very supple with a beautiful translucent quality. We made a book cover with the oak leaves and used the chestnut leaves to make a leaf bowl.

To make a book cover, use diluted PVA, wallpaper paste or double-sided sticky tape to stick the leaves on, and then paint diluted PVA over the top to provide a glossier, stronger finish.

FERN LEAF PAPER

We spread boiled, bleached fern leaves out on the mould with our fingers, moving them around in the water. They made an ornate feathery paper. Make sure you use at least two layers of leaves or else the paper won't hold together. Let the beautiful but fragile paper dry completely before picking it up.

LEAF PLATES AND BOWLS

I couldn't believe it when a friend gave me this beautiful leaf plate – here was a sustainable and biodegradable version of disposable crockery! Leaf plates and bowls like this one are made in India, where they are widely used at festivals and weddings.

Large leaves gathered from the forest are stitched into rounds with fine stems and threads, and then left to dry in the sun before pressing. We made our own papier-mâché version of a leaf bowl, which has been much admired. The leaves were a little reluctant to stick at first, but we sandwiched them tightly together between two bowls and found a way to make it work.

What you need

- Two plastic bowls or plates of the same size
- PVA glue or wallpaper paste, an old paintbrush and some cling film
- A selection of autumn leaves – press them between paper for a couple of days to make them softer and easier to work with
- Weights or stones

MAKING THE BOWL

- Cover the outside of one plastic bowl and the inside of the other with cling film.
- Mix some PVA glue with the same quantity of water. We have also tried sticking the leaves together with wallpaper paste, which is easier to use than PVA, but makes the leaves more brittle, so if you use this, paint the finished bowl with diluted PVA to make it stronger.
- Select some leaves and paint both sides with glue.
- Take the plastic bowl with cling film on its outer side and cover it in overlapping layers of glued leaves, letting the tips stand up above the rim of the bowl.

- When you have several layers of leaves, place the leaf-coated bowl inside the other plastic bowl. Put a weight or stone in the top bowl so that the layers are squashed together.
- Once the glue has begun to dry, remove the outer bowl and cling film and leave the outside of the leaf bowl to dry. After a day or two, put it back in the plastic bowl and remove the inner plastic bowl and cling film and leave the inside to dry. Finally remove the leaf bowl completely and leave to dry.
- If you wish, paint with another layer of diluted PVA to make it last a little longer.

BULRUSH DOLLS

At the Wilderness Gathering (see page 157) Connie took part in a workshop led by Nomad Bushcraft, where she made dolls out of bulrush leaves. Bulrush (also known as cattail) leaves are tough and thick – ideal for folding, rolling and twisting. Leaves of other plants, including grasses and sedges, could be used in a similar way.

- Take several long bulrush leaves. Break off five lengths of about 30cm/12in – you can use the distance between your fingertip and elbow as a rough measure.
- To make the doll's arms, hold one end of a leaf in one hand and the middle of the same leaf in the other hand. Now twist the two sides of the leaf simultaneously towards each other, making a rope. Then do the same from the other end, being careful that the first end does not come untwisted. You should finish up with both halves of the leaf twisted, meeting in the centre.
- Tear a 15cm/6in length of leaf and roll it up tightly to make the head.
- Take another 30cm/12in length of leaf, fold it and place the rolled head in the centre of the fold. Slip the prepared arms below the head between the sides of the folded leaf.
- Take another length of leaf and fold it in half. Then hold it in the middle and slide it over one of the doll's shoulders diagonally.

Repeat with another leaf across the other shoulder. This completes the dress.
- Take the piece of leaf left over after making the head and use this as a belt to hold the whole thing together. Tie it round the doll's waist; then twist it into a knot and tuck the ends through the belt to secure.
- Clip the bottom of the skirt so that all the leaves are the same length.
- The final touch is a broom with a twig handle and bulrush leaf broom head. Push the end of the broom through the looped doll's hand. Alternatively, give your doll an umbrella, a light sabre, a sword or whatever takes your fancy.

Try twisting and folding leaves to make other characters and animals; we were also shown how to make a Samurai warrior and Connie had a go at making a horse. Perhaps the dolls could become part of a story, a puppet show or even an animated film.

PEWTER CASTING

This may seem an unlikely and ambitious activity for this
book, but our children so enjoyed making a pewter pendant
around a fire at the beach that we decided to include it.
This is, after all, yet another example of how young people
might enjoy being creative in the great outdoors. The best
place to do this is on a sandy beach where you are permitted
to make fires.

You will need

- Lead-free jewellery-grade pewter in long thin ingots, available at a modest cost from professional art suppliers (e.g. Tiranti)
- Small casting pot
- Heatproof gloves

METAL CASTING

- Heat the pewter in the casting pot over a small fire until it becomes molten. Pewter has a low melting point, which makes it ideal for using in this way.
- Make moulds by pushing shells or other interesting natural shapes into slightly damp sand.
- Wearing heatproof gloves, carefully pour the molten pewter into a sand mould. If you hold a small stick upright in the mould as you pour, it will leave a hole for threading a string through.
- Leave to cool. Don't attempt to move the pendant until it has gone cold and is set completely hard.

Safety tips

- **Only do this activity outdoors.**
- **Use heatproof gloves when handling the casting pot.**
- **This activity should always be supervised by an adult.**
- **See the fire safety tips on page 156.**

FELTING

Felt is a remarkable soft yet durable fabric made by subjecting wool to moisture, heat and pressure until it mats together. One summer Lily became quite an expert, and she even sold a series of framed felt panels at the local art show. She taught her friends the technique and Hannah came home with a purse and hair tie she had made. Their starting point was carded, dyed wool, but we decided to have a go with raw wool scrounged from a local farmer in the late spring, just after shearing.

The children sorted the wool, choosing the cleanest bits and teasing out the strands. They had great fun treading the wool in a bowl of warm soapy water and were surprised to notice how wonderfully soft and clean their feet were from all the lanolin in the wool. If you can't get wool from a farmer, try collecting small amounts from barbed wire fences when out walking, keeping it safe until you've got a bag full.

You will need
- wool
- an old brush with hard bristles
- a flat-bottomed container
- detergent

Felting involves compressing and matting the wool, which reduces its volume enormously, so a good rule of thumb is to prepare much more wool than you think you will need.

same direction. Place another layer on top, with the fibres at right angles to the bottom layer. Then add the final layer, with the fibres running parallel to the bottom layer. Distribute the wool as evenly as you can.

● If you wish to add layers of colour to your felt, do so during this layering stage. Try using natural dyes to colour cleaned wool (see page 120).

● Mix a small quantity of detergent with half a cup of hot water, and pour over the wool. The hot soapy water lubricates the fibres so that they slide together more easily. You should have enough hot water for all the wool to be wet. Press down on the wool until it forms a mat.

● Massage the wool, letting the soap and wool squish up between your fingers (or toes, if making felt on a larger scale); as the wool firms up you can work more vigorously. Keep working until it holds together; then turn it over and work from the other side.

● Once the wool has matted together in a shape just a little smaller than the container, start the rinsing process. Pour cold water over the wool and keep working it.

● Once you are happy with the felt's shape and thickness, let it dry. If you feel it is too loose, continue felting it to make it tighter.

● Take a bundle of wool and tease it into long fibres – a process known as carding. An early method of carding involved using a teasel seed head which, being covered in tiny hooks, effectively disentangled the wool fibres. We used an old hairbrush.

● Place a layer of carded wool in the container, so that the fibres lie roughly in the

MAKING A LEATHER PURSE

At the Wilderness Gathering (see page 157) Connie noticed a stall selling complete leather hides. It was quite an eye-opener for her to see leather in the shape of the animal! After investigating more closely she bought a template for a purse and some soft leather, and that was the last we heard out of her until she appeared with her finished purse. To this day it's much more special to her than any of her shop-bought purses.

What you need

- Piece of soft leather and some templates, as in this photograph
- A bradawl. Connie made her own little bradawl by whittling a piece of wood to make a handle and then asking an adult to push the metal spike into the end
- A large needle and some strong thread
- A leather thong for a loop and a button or piece of horn

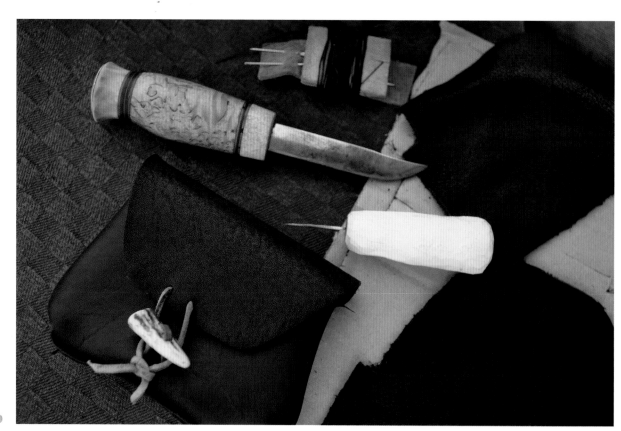

MAKING THE PURSE

- Place the leather on a chopping board. Then place the templates on the leather and cut round them with a sharp knife.
- Use the bradawl to make holes around the sides and bottom of each piece of leather, ready for sewing together.
- Place the leather pieces with their right sides together and sew down each outside edge.
- Turn the purse the right way round and fold the bottom edges together so that they overlap. Sew a double seam along the bottom, as illustrated.
- Sew a button on to the purse. Make a little slit in the lid or sew on a leather loop.

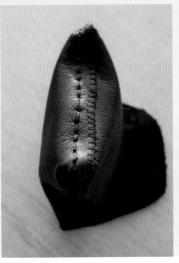

NATURAL MOBILES AND WINDCHIMES

Every Easter we buy a selection of chicken and goose eggs for blowing and decorating, using them to make festive table decorations. One year we discovered that the local farm sold pastel-coloured free-range eggs. We wove three different-sized willow rings, joining them with fine wires into an egg shape.

We made a moss-lined nest filled with chocolate eggs to sit in one of the rings and then added the blown eggs decorated with feathers to make a festive Easter mobile. Pastel-coloured eggs are laid by the Old Cotswold Legbar chickens and are available from many supermarkets as well as local suppliers.

Apart from natural materials all you need to make mobiles is some fine wire, some strong thread and maybe some glue. During the autumn, try making autumn mobiles: perhaps weird animals like this pine pig or this bee-like creature with maple-seed antennae, or little people such as this lady with her pine needle skirt, cone body and rosehip head. And try making mobiles for other festivals such as Christmas or Divali. Or have a go at making natural wind chimes using shells and pebbles to hang outside and remind you of holidays by the sea.

FURTHER INFORMATION

DISCOVERING MORE

LEAVING NO TRACE

FIRE SAFETY

TOOL SAFETY

INDEX

ACKNOWLEDGEMENTS

DISCOVERING MORE ABOUT HOW TO MAKE IT WILD

Some of the activities in this book are covered in more detail in our other books, *Nature's Playground* and *Go Wild!* For more information about these books and other outdoor activities, please visit www.goingwild.net

LEAVING NO TRACE

All the activities in this book should be carried out with the utmost respect for the integrity of wild places and the natural world. Make it wild with minimal impact: respect all wildlife, be considerate to other users, dispose of waste properly and take responsibility for your own actions. Only collect loose and plant materials that are common and found in abundance, and leave wild places as you found them.

FIRE SAFETY

A few of the activities in this book involve the use of fire. Always follow these basic safety tips:

● Make fire on mineral soil, in a pit or a fire pan.
● Don't light a fire in windy or excessively dry weather conditions.
● Never leave a fire unattended.
● Have a supply of water near by in case you need to extinguish the fire or soothe burns.
● Use as little wood as you can and let the fire burn down to ash. Once it is cold remove all traces of your fire.
● Always supervise children and young people when using fire.

TOOL SAFETY

Tool safety is about knowing how to use tools responsibly and appropriately as well as being aware of the potential dangers and how to avoid them.

● Always have a first-aid kit handy and ensure someone present knows how to use it.

● Make sure everyone is aware of the potential dangers of using sharp tools. Accidents usually happen when people are messing around.
● Before using a knife, make sure there is an imaginary 'no entry' zone all around you. To check you have enough space, stand up with your arms spread out and turn around – you shouldn't be able to touch anyone or anything.
● Think about follow-through – in other words, where is your blade likely to go if it slips? Is there anything or anyone in the way?
● Never cut over your lap. The femoral artery in the thigh carries large volumes of blood and if it is severed you can lose a pint of blood a minute.
● Work the blade away from your body, and away from the hand supporting the wood. Never cut towards your hand until you can use it with great control.
● Always cut on to a firm surface such as a steady log.
● If you need to pass a knife to someone else, always do so with the handle pointing towards the other person.
● Always put knives and axes away in their sheaths when not in use; never leave them lying around.
● At the end of each activity session we always collect knives and other tools and put them in a bag together. Young people need to realize that knives should be used only for a craft activity; a knife is a tool and never a weapon.
● Give knives and other sharp tools the respect they deserve: always stick to the rules.

FURTHER INFORMATION ABOUT CREATIVE OUTDOOR ACTIVITIES

Ephemeral art

We recommend looking at the works of ephemeral artists such as Andy Goldsworthy (www.goldsworthy.cc.gla.ac.uk) and Chris Drury (www.chrisdrury.co.uk)

Outdoor toys

Handy website for tools and equipment: www.screwfix.com
Ideas for kite games: www.nafka.net

Make it from clay

Elpel, Thomas J., *Primitive Living, Self-sufficiency and Survival Skills*, The Lyons Press, 2004
Perryman, Jane, *Smoke Firing: Contemporary Artists and Approaches*, A. & C. Black, 2008

Make it with wood

Willow weaving:
www.david.gosling.com
www.wyldwoodwillow.co.uk
Suppliers of willow withies:
www.willowwithies.co.uk
www.windrushwillow.com

Nature's pigments

Dean, Jenny, *Colours from Nature: A Dyer's Handbook*, Search Press, 2009
ISBN 978-0-9530835-2-7

Natural crafts

Lorente, Marie-Jeanne,
The Art of Papermaking with Plants,
Thames and Hudson, 2003
Pewter casting: ingots available from
www.tiranti.co.uk
For further ideas for natural crafts with plants:
www.kew.org and www.edenproject.com

Other useful sources

Organizations that encourage outdoor exploration:

Natural England: an independent public body dedicated to protecting and improving the biodiversity of England's natural environment and encouraging enjoyment of nature.
www.naturalengland.org.uk

The Woodland Trust: the UK's leading woodland conservation charity: its aims include increasing people's understanding and enjoyment of woods.
www.woodlandtrust.org.uk

www.wildlifetrusts.org.uk
www.aonb.org.uk
www.bgci.org
www.forestry.gov.uk
www.playengland.org.uk
www.breathingplaces.org
www.nationaltrust.org.uk

The Wilderness Gathering – the UK's annual bushcraft festival
www.wildernessgathering.co.uk

For information about bushcraft and creative outdoor activities:
www.bisonbushcraft.com
www.islaybirding.co.uk
www.wildwise.co.uk
www.nomad-bushcraft.com
www.naturestrails.co.uk

Podcasts encouraging people to enjoy outdoor lifestyles:
www.theoutdoorsstation.co.uk

INDEX

aboriginal: designs 9, 10, 119; painting 116-118
acorns 37, 110, 121
Afghanistan 62
Alhambra 113
Alsace 113
ash 114, 115, 121
axe 55
axle 50, 52

balloons 5, 61, 66-69
bamboo 62, 63, 67
barbecue 67
bark 55, 121, 133
baskets 93, 102-105
bat: cricket 54-55; rounders 54
beach art 17, 18-21
beads 128, 132
beeswax 89
berries 77, 113, 114, 115, 120, 121
bin liner 65
birch 102, 121
blackthorn pins 27, 29, 80
bleach 136, 137
boats 48, 56-59
body painting 9, 10, 119
boggart 77
book cover 139
bow saw 94
bracken 120
bradawl 103, 130, 132, 150, 151
brake 53
bridle 64
broom 102
bulrush doll 142-143

cairn 22
camera 22
Canada 23, 134
candles 40, 59
carding 148
cattails 142
cave paintings 113
chalk: paint 9, 10, 77, 115, 130, 133; patterns 9, 117
chairs 94-97
charcoal 113, 115
chestnut leaves 139
China 62, 67
Christmas 37, 60, 151
clay 61, 115; firing 81-85; pinch pots 80; puppets 77; sculptures 74, 76, 81; slip 81, 87, 119; tiles 78
colander 136, 137
copper 123
cord 130
corn grains 132
Cornwall 54, 56
cotton 121

deckle 135
detergent 147
Divali 151
dinosaur nest 26

dragon 42, 43
driftwood 54, 129; sculptures 24, 98-99; yacht 56, 57
dustbin 84-85
dyes 120-123

Easter 152
eggs 152-153
elderberry juice 11, 120
ephemeral art 14-45
eucalyptus 102

fabric 121, 123
feathers 73, 77, 115, 129, 131, 133, 153
felting 146-149
fern 136, 139
fire 12, 85, 69, 121, 144, 145; safety 156
fish 19
fishing line 30, 37, 58, 59, 63, 69
flaming balloons 66-69
flyweight envelope stiffener 60
France 113
frog 117
furniture 94

galls 121
glass 130, 133
gliders 60-61
gloves 33, 123, 124
glow sticks 61
go-cart 12, 50-53
grass 115
green man 73, 76
Groombridge gardens 31

hairbrush 148
hair dryer 67
hammer 51, 94, 135
handsaw 51
hazel 102

ice 33-41
incinerator bin 82, 84-85
India 140
indigo 124
Indonesia 56, 62
ingots 145
Inukshuk 23

Japan 62
jewellery 130-133

Kalahari 129
kangaroo 116, 117
kiln 82-85
kites 62-65
knife 63, 151; safety 156

lanterns: flaming 66-69; ice 40-41; snow 44-45; withy 106-108
leaf: boats 9, 57; bowls 139, 140-141; flames 29; kite 62; pictures 27-29; plates 140; poems 30; snake 29

leather purse 150-151
leaves 77, 79, 80, 121, 136, 140-141, 142
leaving no trace 156
locking nuts 51
loppers 94
luminous fishing lures 61

madder 121
marotte puppet 77
masking tape 63, 89, 107, 108
mermaid 19
mesh 135
methylated spirits 67, 69
mint 113
mobiles 152-153
modifiers 121
monster 24, 76
mordant 121
moss 115
mould 37, 135

nail 94, 99, 121
nettle: cord 130; paper 138
newspaper 89, 136, 137
nightlights 40, 44, 45, 59, 107
nuts 26, 51

oak 121, 139
ochre 113
outdoor toys 48-69

paints 113, 114-119
paintbrushes 107, 114, 140
pallet 50, 51
paper making 134-139
papier-mâché 140
pebbles 21, 129, 130
pendant 130, 133
pestle and mortar 114, 115, 120, 123
pewter 144-145
pinch pots 80
planes 60-61
plaster of Paris 79
plastic: bag 65; washer 51, 52
plasticine 37
Polynesia 62
poppy seedhead 132
pulp 137
puppets 77
PVA glue 63, 67, 78, 106, 107, 108, 133, 139, 140,
    141
pyrograph pen 130, 132

rafts 58
rhubarb root 121, 123, 124
rods: weaving 103, 104, 105; structural 103, 104, 105
rosehips 132
rubber gloves 123, 136, 139
rubbish sculpture 24

safety: fire 156; tools 156
salt 87

San people 129
sand: castle 17; painting 16, 19; sculptures 19;
    silhouettes 6-7, 10, 18
saucepans 136
sawdust 85, 89
seaweed 87, 99
secateurs 100, 101, 103, 105, 107, 136
seeds 26, 40, 79, 129, 130, 132, 152
scissors 56, 67, 107, 136
screws 52, 60, 61
sculpture: clay 76, 81; driftwood 98-99; ice 38-39;
    rubbish 24-25; sand 19; snow 32, 33, 42-45;
    stone 23; twig 100-101
shadows 22
shells 20, 37, 79, 80, 99, 121, 130, 133, 145
sieve 123, 136, 137
silk 121
smoke decorating 86-89
soapbox derby 50
Spain 113
spider's web 31
staple gun 135
stone: cairns 22; mermaid 23; patterns 21;
    pictures 20; sculpture 23; towers 21
string 34, 36, 54, 56, 58, 79, 87
sunbeams 31

tampon 69
teasels 148
templates 150, 151
thermal mittens 85
tide 17, 18, 21
tie dye 124
tissue paper 63, 64, 67, 68, 107, 108
toothbrush 79, 81
tree ring 26
troll 73
turmeric 121
turtle 19
twine 55

u-bolt 50, 52

vinegar 121, 123

wallpaper paste 140
walnut 121
washing soda 121, 123, 136, 137
wasps' nest 134
whale 20
wheels 50, 51, 52, 53
whittling 93
willow: 65, 67, 121; baskets 93; bat 54, 55;
    puppets 100; weaving 100, 101
Wilderness Gathering 157
wind chimes 152
wire 67, 69
withy lanterns 106-109
woodland art 26-31
wool 123, 147-149
Wyldwood Willow 93

ACKNOWLEDGEMENTS

Thanks to everyone who has shared ideas and provided
practical advice and support. Please notify the publisher if
there are inadvertent omissions in these acknowledgements,
which will be rectified in future editions.

We would like to thank the following people for their help
and advice: Jane and Bob White; Carol Harris; Jeremy Hastings
(Islay Birding), Chris Holland and Chris Salisbury (Wildwise),
Jon-Paul Lamoureux, Amanda (Wyldwood Willow) and every-
one else who shared ideas with us at the 2008 Wilderness
Gathering; Jenny Dean; David Gosling; David Millin,
Martin Maudsley; Michelle Kitto; Helen and James Jackson;
Heather Frances; Nigel Adams; Bill Hoare; Kate Cheng;
Kate Castleden; Selma Smyly; Louise Robinson; Iain Naismith;
Rod Anderson Boyle; Alex Travers; Ollie Rathmill; and the many
families and friends who have supported us in so many ways.

A big thank-you to all the young people who took part in
activities: Tom U; Jonathon and Jessie A; Lily, Charlie and
Toby R; Agnes K; Carolyn S; Clifford, Frankie and Anya C;
Anna, Tim, Nicholas and Ella V; Alice F; Fiona and Eliza N;
Tilly S; Lucas R; Rebecca and Edward W; Harry G; Alexander B;
Matt, Tris and Will E; Natasha and Adam H; Anna, Laura and
Ben W; Sophie T; Isabella G; Catherine F; Milly B; Tilly G;
Rebecca M; Lydia, Helena and Lucian S, David C; Milly H;
Christopher and Sienna W; Scott H; Ama and Mahalia J; Danny,
Jess and Natali K; Kate W; Tsering L; Ella W; Jess R; Rose P.

Many thanks to our husbands, Ben and Peter, and our children,
Jake, Dan, Connie, Hannah and Edward, for all their support and
patience. And finally, thanks to everyone at Frances Lincoln
who has helped *Make it Wild!* become a reality.